Apress Pocket Guides

Apress Pocket Guides present concise summaries of cutting-edge developments and working practices throughout the tech industry. Shorter in length, books in this series aim to deliver quick-to-read guides that are easy to absorb, perfect for the time-poor professional.

This series covers the full spectrum of topics relevant to the modern industry, from security, AI, machine learning, cloud computing, web development, product design, to programming techniques and business topics too.

Typical topics might include:

- A concise guide to a particular topic, method, function or framework

- Professional best practices and industry trends

- A snapshot of a hot or emerging topic

- Industry case studies

- Concise presentations of core concepts suited for students and those interested in entering the tech industry

- Short reference guides outlining 'need-to-know' concepts and practices.

More information about this series at https://link.springer.com/book-series/17385

Secure Boot Encryption with Linux

Implementation for Embedded Developers

Rodolfo Giometti

Apress®

Secure Boot Encryption with Linux: Implementation for Embedded Developers

Rodolfo Giometti
LUCCA, Italy

ISBN-13 (pbk): 979-8-8688-2817-1   ISBN-13 (electronic): 979-8-8688-2818-8
https://doi.org/10.1007/979-8-8688-2818-8

Managing Director, Apress Media LLC: Welmoed Spahr
Acquisitions Editor: James Robinson-Prior
Editorial Project Manager: Gryffin Winkler

Cover designed by eStudioCalamar

Distributed to the book trade worldwide by Springer Science+Business Media New York, 1 New York Plaza, New York, NY 10004. Phone 1-800-SPRINGER, fax (201) 348-4505, e-mail orders-ny@springer-sbm.com, or visit www.springeronline.com. Apress Media, LLC is a Delaware LLC and the sole member (owner) is Springer Science + Business Media Finance Inc (SSBM Finance Inc). SSBM Finance Inc is a **Delaware** corporation.

For information on translations, please e-mail booktranslations@springernature.com; for reprint, paperback, or audio rights, please e-mail bookpermissions@springernature.com.

Apress titles may be purchased in bulk for academic, corporate, or promotional use. eBook versions and licenses are also available for most titles. For more information, reference our Print and eBook Bulk Sales web page at http://www.apress.com/bulk-sales.

Any source code or other supplementary material referenced by the author in this book is available to readers on GitHub. For more detailed information, please visit https://www.apress.com/gp/services/source-code.

If disposing of this product, please recycle the paper

In memory of my Grandma Dina

Table of Contents

About the Author

Rodolfo Giometti is an engineer, IT specialist, embedded GNU/Linux expert, and Software Libre evangelist. He has over 20 years of experience with GNU/Linux Embedded on x86, ARM, MIPS- and PowerPC-based platforms, and he is the maintainer of the LinuxPPS projects (the Linux's Pulse Per Second subsystem). Rodolfo still actively contributes to the Linux source code contributing several patches and new device drivers for industrial applications.

About the Technical Reviewers

Antonio Tringali is an engineer specializing in embedded systems, industrial electronics, and energy market analytics. His work spans firmware architecture, Linux-based systems, and secure system design. He combines rigorous engineering practice with a strong focus on reliability and cybersecurity.

With over 45 years of experience in firmware and software development, numerical analysis, and hardware design, **Giacomo Vianelli** specializes in the design and architecture of secure devices. He currently serves as CTO and Head of R&D, while actively contributing to technical committees focused on the development and implementation of industry standards. Throughout his extensive career, he has gained profound expertise in the industrial sector, focusing on the design and development of complex systems such as Intelligent Electronic Devices (IEDs), Remote Terminal Units (RTUs), and Distributed Control Systems (DCS) for the power, oil and gas, and energy industries.

Acknowledgments

Heartfelt thanks to my technical reviewers, Antonio Tringali and Giacomo Vianelli, for their suggestions and critical reading of what is reported in this book.

This book would not be the same without the intuition of James Robinson-Prior and the support of Gryffin Winkler and Shobana Srinivasan.

Finally, to my family for their unwavering support throughout this journey. To my spouse Valentina, and my children Romina and Raffaele, who supported me during the time of writing this book.

Introduction

Modern Linux-based embedded systems—from industrial control units and automotive platforms to high-value IoT devices—represent the front lines of digital security. Yet, many rely on security models that fail due to not strengthening security implementations. The moment a sophisticated adversary compromises a bootloader or an operating system to gain root privileges, the control of the machine is typically lost. Encryption keys, system secrets, and code integrity are instantly exposed, compromising the entire device. For mission-critical products, this is an unacceptable vulnerability.

This book is your definitive technical guide to moving beyond traditional security measures to build a system where integrity and secrets are root-proof. The goal is to empower you to deliver products with a provable, uncompromisable Chain-of-Trust and secured encryption key protection.

What This Book Covers

This book begins by showing how to leverage the **Linux Key-Management Facility (Keyring)** to manage the most sensitive cryptographic material, sealing the keys so they cannot be read or exposed, even if an attacker successfully gains full root access. Standard keys in Linux will be introduced, but vendor-specific key management solutions with interesting features will also be considered. It will then move on to illustrate some typical uses of these keys for secure boot.

It will then move on to a detailed description of what secure boot is (and what it is not), describing how the **Chain-of-Trust** works and what a secure boot sequence should look like. Not only that, but it will also analyze issues related to the production of new systems, as well as how to distribute updates while always respecting what a good secure boot system should do.

Although the secure boot implementation is highly vendor-specific, the final section of this book will attempt to demonstrate, as generally as possible, how real-world implementations might work: one with the **Rescue boot** schema and one with the **A/B boot** schema.

As a final addition, this book will also present some ideas on how a good tamper prevention system working with Secure Boot should work and some considerations about the bootloader environment management.

Below is a brief introduction of each chapter:

- *Chapter 1—Linux Cryptography*: This chapter serves as the foundational layer, explaining how the Linux kernel's cryptographic subsystem works. It introduces the difference between **signature keys** (used for integrity and authenticity verification, central to Secure Boot) and **encryption keys** (used for confidentiality), and then it presents the **Linux Key-Management Facility (Keyring)**—the secure repository for cryptographic keys within the kernel. The chapter provides an in-depth explanation of user keys, trusted keys, etc., detailing how they are integrated with hardware (e.g., like a TPM, OPTEE, and other security devices) to prevent key exposure even if an attacker gains root privileges. Readers will learn the practical steps and kernel interactions necessary to store, manage, and utilize secrets in a way that makes them inaccessible to compromised user-space processes.

- *Chapter 2—What the Secure Boot Is (and What It Is NOT)*: This is a critical chapter focusing on the core mechanism for root-proof security via the Secure Boot mechanism. It presents the concept of **Chain-of-Trust** in detail and shows how it works in each step of the booting process for a Linux-based system. This chapter also explains how the factory production and system update procedures should be implemented in order to be compatible with the Chain-of-Trust requirements.

- *Chapter 3—Real Implementations*: This chapter presents a real implementation of the Chain-of-Trust in two different scenarios: the **Rescue** schema (where we need a reliable way to restore the factory conditions) and the **A/B** schema (where we need to update the system while it is running). The chapter explains how a normal boot works, how a factory production may work, and how a system update may be implemented in both cases.

- *Chapter 4—Final Considerations*: This chapter provides practical examples for the effective generation of encryption and signing keys for two specific real-world CPUs (i.MX and STM32MP1 series) that use two different mechanisms to store system secrets: the **Fuse-Centric and Hybrid approach**, along with a discussion of potential licensing issues developers may encounter when designing a secure system.

Then a brief introduction of the appendixes:

- *Appendix A: Notes on Tamper Detection*: Even if the tamper detection is not part of the secure boot, it is undoubtedly strictly related. In fact, CPUs that support this feature usually, when a tamper event occurs, stop the boot sequence (and all keys are zeroed). That's why we have added this appendix where we will present some ideas about how a **tamper event** should be managed within the secure boot.

- *Appendix B: Securing Secrets Across Booting Stages*: In this appendix, we will present some possible issues regarding the **U-Boot environment**, which is a plain text memory area that can interact with the following stages (such as the kernel or the user space applications). Due to its unsecure nature, it can be used to exploit the Chain-of-Trust if not correctly managed.

What You Will Learn

By the time you finish this book, you will possess the advanced technical knowledge and practical skills to design, implement, and maintain a high-assurance, secure embedded Linux system. Specifically, you will learn to

- *Utilize the Linux Key-Management Facility (Keyring)*: Learn to implement and manage cryptographic secrets using the kernel's secure Keyring, ensuring keys are inaccessible to user space processes, even those with root privileges.

- *Employ the Linux Crypto API*: Understand and utilize the kernel's cryptographic subsystem via interfaces like the AF_ALG socket for secure hashing, signing, and encryption operations with potential hardware acceleration.

- *Establish an Unbreakable Chain-of-Trust*: Meticulously implement a Chain-of-Trust that verifies the integrity and authenticity of every system component, from the initial hardware Root-of-Trust and the pre-bootloader (e.g., U-Boot SPL) to the final Linux kernel load.

- *Achieve Transparent Full-Disk Encryption*: Integrate the secure Keyring with technologies like dm-crypt to encrypt the root filesystem, ensuring data confidentiality for the entire operating system while securely managing the keys at the kernel level.

- *Understand precisely what the Linux Secure Boot implementation is*: This allow you to correctly design defenses against sophisticated threats like persistent bootkits and malicious code injection.

Written for the experienced embedded Linux developers and security architects, this is more than an overview—it is a technical manual. By mastering the low-level hardware, bootloader, and kernel-centric techniques detailed within these pages, you will be equipped to build Linux-based products that are resilient against the most sophisticated bootkits and unauthorized code execution.

What You Need for This Book

The following are the prerequisites for efficient learning.

Software Prerequisite

Regarding the software, you should know the C language and have some skills in Bash and Python.

Most examples have been done in Ubuntu 22.04, but you can also use a newer Ubuntu Long-Term Support (LTS) or a Debian-based system too with little modifications. Alternatively, you may use another GNU/Linux distribution, but with a little effort from you, mainly regarding the needed tools' installation, library dependencies, and package management. Practical examples done within embedded systems have been implemented for Yocto Scarthgap, but you can use any newer release.

Foreign systems such as Windows, macOS, or similar are not covered in this book.

Hardware Prerequisite

In this book, we have used both a normal PC-x86 at 64 bits to build code and three embedded systems based on CPUs iMX8 (equipped with the CAAM device), iMX9, and STM32MP1; however, you can use another embedded kit with Yocto (or a suitable embedded distribution) to reproduce what is present in the book (except when the CAAM is required, of course; in these cases you must use a CAAM-equipped CPU).

Conventions

In this book, you will find many text styles that distinguish between different kinds of information. Here are some examples of these styles and an explanation of their meaning.

Long Outputs, Codes, and Command Lines

When I need to show part of long outputs (or file contents), I may snip non-relevant text by replacing it with three dots, leaving untouched the important content, as in the example below:

```
$ cat very_long_file.txt
Line 1
Line 2
Line 3
...
Line 999
Line 1000
...
```

In the above output, lines after `Line 3` until `Line 999` have been snipped, as well as lines after `Line 1000`.

Code words in text, folder names, filenames, file extensions, path names, dummy URLs, and user input are shown as follows: "To get the preceding kernel messages, we can use both the `dmesg` and `tail -f /var/log/kern.log` commands."

A block of code is set as follows:

```
#include <stdio.h>
int main(int argc, char *argv[])
{
        printf("Hello World!\n");
        return 0;
}
```

where the indentation can be composed of eight or four spaces in order to get the best readability.

Any command line—in both cases I need to issue a privileged or non-privileged command—is written as follows:

```
$ cat /etc/lsb-release
```

This is because this condition may vary. You should issue the proper command as the root user or via `sudo` when requested by your system.

Note also that due to space reasons in the book, you may read very long command lines as follows:

```
$ echo "Very secret message" | openssl enc -aes-256-cbc -e -K 0123
456789abcdef0123456789abcdef0123456789abcdef0123456789abcdef -iv 0
123456789abcdef0123456789abcdef > /tmp/secret.enc
```

However, generally, for better readability, I'll break the command line as below:

```
$ echo "Very secret message" | \
    openssl enc -aes-256-cbc -e \
    -K 0123456789abcdef0123456789abcdef0123456789abcdef01
    23456789abcdef \
    -iv 0123456789abcdef0123456789abcdef > /tmp/secret.enc
```

However, in some special cases you can find broken output lines as follows:

```
$ openssl dgst -sha256 < /tmp/id.txt
SHA2-256(stdin)= 5e2ea0c72053ce80c13549b2c6e3365098d5b
c61015b39908c78709
0f70189d9
```

Unfortunately, these lines cannot be easily reported into a printed book, so you should consider them as a single line.

Other Conventions

New terms and important words are shown in **bold** or *italic*. Words that you see on the screen, for example, in menus or dialog boxes, appear in the text like this: `Clicking the Next button moves you to the next screen string`.

Warnings or significant notes appear in a box like this:

Tips and tricks appear like this.

CHAPTER 1

Linux Cryptography

The Linux kernel incorporates a robust and versatile **cryptographic subsystem**. This subsystem provides a comprehensive suite of cryptographic primitives and algorithms, acting as a foundational security layer for the entire system. By implementing these functions directly within the kernel, Linux ensures that crucial cryptographic operations, such as data encryption, secure hashing, etc., are performed with hardware acceleration (if available) and are readily available to various kernel components and user-space applications. This is vital for securing everything from network communications and filesystems to system integrity.

Strictly connected with the cryptographic subsystem is the **kernel keyring**, which acts as a secure repository for cryptographic keys, allowing for the safe management and sharing of these keys among kernel processes and modules and user-space processes.

Before seeing these components in detail, we need to introduce some basic cryptographic concepts in order to have a common basic knowledge of some terms.

1.1 Signature Keys vs. Encryption Keys

In cryptography, the use of **signature keys** or **encryption keys** is intended for two different purposes. The former are used to ensure authenticity and integrity; that is, the goal is to verify who sent the data and that the data

© Rodolfo Giometti 2026

R. Giometti, *Secure Boot Encryption with Linux*, Apress Pocket Guides,
https://doi.org/10.1007/979-8-8688-2818-8_1

has not been altered since it was signed. While the latter are used to ensure confidentiality, so the goal is to make data unreadable to anyone except the intended recipient.

To do a digital signature, we must use an asymmetric key pair, while for encryption, we can use *asymmetric* or *symmetric encryption.*

As the reader may argue, for asymmetric encryption we must use an asymmetric key pair, while for symmetric encryption we must use a symmetric key.

However, due to speed issues, all CPUs use symmetric encryption for securing their code, so from now until the end of this book, we are going to use symmetric encryption only.

In cryptography there are tons of signature and encryption methods; however, for our purposes, for encryption we will use the **Advanced Encryption Standard–Cipher Block Chaining (AES-CBC).**

Cipher Block Chaining (CBC) is a mode of operation for block ciphers. It addresses a weakness of simple block ciphers, where identical plain text blocks would produce identical ciphertext blocks, while, in CBC, each block of plain text is XORed with the previous ciphertext block before it's encrypted.

In simple terms, AES-256 provides the powerful *scrambling.* That's why it is one of the most widely used encryption algorithms.

While for signature we are going to use the **Elliptic Curve Digital Signature Algorithm (ECDSA)** that is based on **Elliptic Curve Cryptography (ECC),** which offers greater efficiency and smaller key sizes compared to other signature algorithms (like, e.g., RSA that relies on the difficulty of factoring large numbers instead) with the **SHA-256 (Secure Hash Algorithm 256-bit)**, which is a cryptographic hash function that produces a unique, fixed-size 256-bit hash (the hashing function is needed to obtain a unique representation of a file where the signature is effectively computed).

> Even if we are going to focus our discussions on these algorithms only, the readers should be able to use other algorithms with a little effort.

Usually, on Linux-based systems, these algorithms can be used with the **OpenSSL** tool (`https://github.com/openssl/openssl`). For example, to encrypt a file, we can use the following command:

```
$ echo "Very secret message" | \
    openssl enc -aes-256-cbc -e \
    -K 0123456789abcdef0123456789abcdef0123456789abcdef0123456
    789abcdef \
    -iv 0123456789abcdef0123456789abcdef > /tmp/secret.enc
$ hexdump -v /tmp/secret.enc
0000000 a1e7 1fa6 ad8c 1825 c4ba 599d 7629 f3f2
0000010 fa9f f0f0 4c73 5f35 8fe4 d5ac 7b3f 9960
0000020
$ cat /tmp/secret.enc | \
    openssl enc -aes-256-cbc -d \
    -K 0123456789abcdef0123456789abcdef0123456789abcdef01234567
    89abcdef \
    -iv 0123456789abcdef0123456789abcdef
Very secret message
```

In the example, the string `Very secret message` has been encrypted via the AES-CBC at 256 bits (`aes-256-cbc`) algorithm and by using the encryption key and initial vectors specified with the option arguments `-K` and `-iv`, respectively.

Note that in the first `openssl` execution, we used the `-e` option argument to do an *encryption*, while in the second command, we used the `-d` option argument to do a *decryption*.

Another example can be how to use OpenSSL to hash a file:

```
$ echo "My name is Rodolfo Giometti" > /tmp/id.txt
$ openssl dgst -sha256 /tmp/id.txt
SHA2-256(/tmp/id.txt)= 5e2ea0c72053ce80c13549b2c6e3365098d5bc
61015b39908
c787090f70189d9
```

If we alter the file a bit, the hash function output changes, giving a very different value:

```
$ echo "My name is Rodolfo Gionetti" > /tmp/id.txt
$ openssl dgst -sha256 /tmp/id.txt
SHA2-256(/tmp/id.txt)= c7d8444dc37a87269735d52c0f39c5181689e
9a68b786eed7
09f42b24318eb56
```

This is a specific feature of every hashing function, that is: *if the input changes for just one bit, the output must entirely change.*

OpenSSL can also be used to get random values as shown below:

```
$ openssl rand 32 | od -tx1
0000000 23 83 28 06 e3 b8 14 21 5a 95 8a b7 37 a8 28 e1
0000020 26 cf 28 e5 24 8d 0d 92 a6 f5 a6 a9 c6 83 22 b2
0000040
```

```
$ openssl rand 32 | od -tx1
0000000 95 2d b0 9b 2e 5f 11 21 a6 90 50 ad ef fe 44 d2
0000020 9e 15 26 08 17 58 0b 60 6a 38 66 ca 77 ac 1a 3c
0000040
```

The OpenSSL toolkit is really a great package for crypto applications, but we are going to see that to solve specific security problems, especially the hardware-related ones, we may need different tools. In fact, regarding the above encryption/decryption commands, we have to specify the key in the command line (or from a file), which exposes the key to everyone who has access to the root filesystem (with the right privileges, of course).

In this book, we are going to see several ways to prevent the key from being read even if a process has the root privileges!

1.2 The Linux Crypto API

The Linux Crypto API is a cryptography framework built into Linux that provides a consistent interface for the kernel to use a wide variety of cryptographic algorithms and functions. Furthermore, it provides a uniform interface for different algorithms in such a way that a kernel module or user-space application can request an algorithm like AES-CBC or SHA256 without needing to know the specifics of its implementation. For example, we can see the list of all available algorithms in an iMX8-based system by inspecting the virtual file /proc/crypto, as shown below (this output has been captured on an iMX8-based system):

```
# cat /proc/crypto
...
name        : tk(cbc(aes))
driver      : tk-cbc-aes-caam
module      : kernel
priority    : 3000
```

```
refcnt        : 2
selftest      : passed
internal      : no
type          : skcipher
async         : yes
blocksize     : 16
min keysize   : 36
max keysize   : 164
ivsize        : 16
chunksize     : 16
walksize      : 16

name          : cbc(aes)
driver        : cbc-aes-caam
module        : kernel
priority      : 3000
refcnt        : 1
selftest      : passed
internal      : no
type          : skcipher
async         : yes
blocksize     : 16
min keysize   : 16
max keysize   : 32
ivsize        : 16
chunksize     : 16
walksize      : 16
...
name          : cbc(aes)
driver        : cbc-aes-ce
module        : kernel
priority      : 300
```

```
refcnt        : 1
selftest      : passed
internal      : no
type          : skcipher
async         : no
blocksize     : 16
min keysize   : 16
max keysize   : 32
ivsize        : 16
chunksize     : 16
walksize      : 16
...
```

This file shows all the algorithm names (the label name), their type (the label type, which in our example the type skcipher stands for *symmetric key ciphers*), and other details such as

- name: The generic name of the cipher that is subject to the priority-based selection (see below). This name can be used by the cipher allocation API calls (all names listed above are examples of such generic names).

- driver: The unique name of the cipher. Even this name can be used by the cipher allocation API calls.

- module: The kernel module providing the cipher implementation (or kernel for statically linked ciphers).

- priority: The priority value of the cipher implementation (see below).

- refcnt: The reference count of the respective cipher, that is, the number of current consumers of this cipher.

- selftest: Whether the self-test for the cipher has been passed or not.

- `blocksize`: Blocksize of cipher in bytes.

- `min keysize`/`max keysize`: min/max key size in bytes.

- `ivsize`: Initial vectors (IV) size in bytes.

- `seedsize`: Required size of seed data for random number generator.

- `digestsize`: Output size of the message digest for hashing algorithms.

See the file `Documentation/crypto/architecture.rst` in the Linux kernel sources for a complete list.

The priority-based selection is a way to select the best available implementation for a requested algorithm. When we ask for a generic algorithm name, the kernel automatically selects the one with the highest priority.

In the above content for the `/proc/crypto` file, we can see two algorithms with the same `cbc(aes)` name; however, one has the following properties:

```
name         : cbc(aes)
driver       : cbc-aes-caam
module       : kernel
priority     : 3000
```

While the other one has:

```
name         : cbc(aes)
driver       : cbc-aes-ce
module       : kernel
priority     : 300
```

As we can see, they are two different implementations of the same AES-CBC algorithm due to the fact each has its driver; however, the former has a higher priority of 3000. In this scenario, if we ask for the `cbc(aes)` algorithm, the kernel uses the one with the higher priority, in our example the one implemented by the driver `cbc-aes-caam` (if multiple implementations have the same highest priority, the kernel's behavior is typically to select one arbitrarily).

We are going to explain what the CAAM is below in this section, since it will be used to explain different and fascinating cryptographic solutions. For the moment, the readers should consider it as an alternate algorithm implementation within the kernel.

To override this priority-based selection, we must ask for the unique name (i.e., the driver name) instead of the generic name; the kernel will use that specific implementation regardless of its priority. In our example, we must ask for `cbc-aes-ce` to select the other implementation (we are going to provide an example of this mechanism below in this section).

All cryptographic algorithms listed within `/proc/crypto` can be used within the kernel for special tasks (not reported in this book) or in user space by using the **AF_ALG socket** interface. This interface allows developers to directly talk to the underlying crypto layer (software or hardware, according to each priority). In the `socket()` system call manpages (`man 2 socket`), we can read the following information:

```
SOCKET(2)        Linux Programmer's Manual        SOCKET(2)
NAME
       socket - create an endpoint for communication

SYNOPSIS
       #include <sys/types.h>          /* See NOTES */
       #include <sys/socket.h>
```

```
int socket(int domain, int type, int protocol);
```

DESCRIPTION

socket() creates an endpoint for communication and returns a file descriptor that refers to that endpoint. The file descriptor returned by a successful call will be the lowest-numbered file descriptor not currently open for the process.

The domain argument specifies a communication domain; this selects the protocol family which will be used for communication.
These families are defined in <sys/socket.h>. The formats currently understood by the Linux kernel include:

```
Name            Purpose                         Man page
AF_UNIX         Local communication             unix(7)
...

AF_ALG          Interface to kernel crypto API
...
```

Stating this information, an elementary example of how to define such a kind of socket is reported below:

```
static int set_afalg_socket(..., char *key, size_t key_len)
{
        int s;
        struct sockaddr_alg sa = {
                .salg_family = AF_ALG,
                .salg_type = "skcipher",
                .salg_name = "cbc(aes)",
        };
```

```c
    int ret;

    ret = socket(AF_ALG, SOCK_SEQPACKET, 0);
    if (ret < 0)
            ("socket(AF_ALG): %m");
    s = ret;

    ret = bind(s, (struct sockaddr *) &sa, sizeof(sa));
    if (ret < 0)
            fatal("bind(): %m");

    ret = setsockopt(s, SOL_ALG, ALG_SET_KEY, key,
    key_len);
    if (ret < 0)
            fatal("setsockopt(ALG_SET_KEY): %m");

    ret = accept(s, NULL, 0);
    if (ret < 0)
            fatal("accept(): %m");
    close(s);

    return ret;
}
```

Everything is defined within the structure sockaddr_alg above: in
salg_family, we specify the protocol family (which is AF_ALG), and in
salg_type, we set the required logic from the kernel (in our example, we
set skcipher to enable the symmetric cipher logic). But, as seen above,
we can also specify types, such as hash for the hash logic, rng for random
number generator, etc. (further information about this mechanism can be
found at https://www.kernel.org/doc/html/v6.11/crypto/userspace-
if.html).

In order to use this API, we can use OpenSSL with the option `-engine afalg` as below:

```
$ echo "Very secret message" | \
    openssl enc -engine afalg -aes-256-cbc -e \
    -K 0123456789abcdef0123456789abcdef0123456789abcdef01234567
    89abcdef \
    -iv 0123456789abcdef0123456789abcdef > /dev/null
Engine "afalg" set.
```

If we get no error, the encryption has been done inside the kernel. To verify it (if we don't trust the message `Engine "afalg" set.`), we can use the `strace` command as shown below:

```
$ echo "Very secret message" | \
    strace openssl enc -engine afalg -aes-256-cbc -e \
    -K 0123456789abcdef0123456789abcdef0123456789abcdef012345678
    9abcdef \
    -iv 0123456789abcdef0123456789abcdef > /dev/null
...
socket(AF_ALG, SOCK_SEQPACKET, 0)          = 3
bind(3, {sa_family=AF_ALG, salg_type="skcipher", salg_feat=0,
salg_mask=0, salg_name="cbc(aes)"}, 88) = 0
accept(3, NULL, NULL)                      = 4
setsockopt(3, SOL_ALG, ALG_SET_KEY, "\1#Eg\211\253\315\357\1#
Eg\211\253\31
5\357\1#Eg\211\253\315\357\1#Eg\211\253\315\357", 32) = 0
io_setup(1, [0x77ab6c99f000])              = 0
newfstatat(0, "", {st_mode=S_IFIFO|0600, st_size=0, ...},
AT_EMPTY_PATH) = 0
read(0, "Very secret message\n", 8192)  = 20
read(0, "", 4096)                          = 0
```

```
sendmsg(4, {msg_name=NULL, msg_namelen=0, msg_iov=[{iov_
base="Very secret mess", iov_len=16}], msg_iovlen=1, msg_
control=[{cmsg_len=20, cmsg_level=SOL_ALG, cmsg_type=0x3},
{cmsg_len=36, cmsg_level=SOL_ALG, cmsg_type=0x2}], msg_
controllen=64, msg_flags=MSG_MORE}, 0) = 16
...
```

Above we can see:

- The `socket()` call with the `AF_ALG` domain

- The `bind()` call with `sa_family` set to `AF_ALG`, `salg_type` set to `skcipher`, and `salg_name` equal to `cbc(aes)` to set the encryption algorithm

- The `setsockopt()` call with `ALG_SET_KEY` to set the encryption key

- The `sendmsg()` call used to send the data to be encrypted to the kernel

Readers should now note that in this case we do several system calls that degrade the encryption speed. To properly estimate encryption speed, we can do this simple test. First, we create a big file:

```
$ dd if=/dev/zero of=/tmp/dummyfile.bin bs=1M count=1000
```

Then we can use the `time` command to measure encryption speed all in user space, as reported below:

```
$ time openssl enc -aes-256-cbc -pbkdf2 \
    -k "dummy_passphrase" -in /tmp/dummyfile.bin \
    -out /tmp/dummyfile.bin.enc

real    0m2,881s
user    0m1,036s
sys     0m1,842s
```

Then we can repeat the measure when the kernel crypto API is used:

```
$ time openssl enc -engine afalg -aes-256-cbc -pbkdf2 \
    -k "dummy_passphrase" -in /tmp/dummyfile.bin \
    -out /tmp/dummyfile.bin.enc
Engine "afalg" set.

real    0m4,250s
user    0m0,232s
sys     0m3,988s
```

It's easy to see that when we select the *afalg* engine, the (usually) decreases due to the numerous system calls we need to pass data back and forth with the kernel.

However, in this book, the real problem is not focused on *speed* but on *security* instead! In fact, our main goal is to obtain a secure system (if the system is also quick, it's better, but it's not a mandatory requirement)! To obtain this target, we have to introduce another tool that uses the crypto API by default to do cryptographic activities and that adds the Linux keyring management. This tool is named **crypto-afalg** and it can be retrieved at `https://github.com/giometti/crypto-afalg`.

The advantage of using this tool is that by using it, we can specify which is the encryption key in several ways. If we take a look at the usage message, we see the following output:

```
$ crypto-afalg -h
usage: crypto-afalg [ -d|--debug ] [ -h|--help ] [--version]
[ --force-d
river <name> ] <command> ...
  <command> can be:
    encrypt <algo> <opts> : encrypt data
    decrypt <algo> <opts> : decrypt data
    hash <algo> <opts>    : compute data hash
```

Regarding the decrypt subcommand we have the following information:

```
$ crypto-afalg decrypt -h
to see available algos use:
        crypto-afalg decrypt
to check a kernel algo use:
        crypto-afalg decrypt check-kalgo <kname>
to get help use:
        crypto-afalg decrypt help|-h|--help
normal usage:
        crypto-afalg decrypt <algo> <KEY> <IV> | <PASS> [
        <SALT> ] [ -i|--iterations <val> ]
where <KEY> can be one of:
    -K|--key <val>          : hex value key
    -k|--keyfile <name>     : key from file
    -S|--keyserial <val>    : key from keyring
where <IV> can be one of:
    -V|--iv <str>           : iv
    -v|--ivfile <name>      : iv from file
where <PASS> can be one of:
    -P|--pass <str>         : passkey
    -p|--passfile <name>    : passkey from file
where <SALT> can be one of:
    -T|--salt <str>         : salt
    -t|--saltfile <name>    : salt from file
NOTE: keyring key can be:
        - a simple serial number, or
        - a symbolic name as [<keyring>,]<type>,<name>
```

In the above output, we see that by using the -S option argument, we can specify a key by using its serial number within the Linux keyring. And this is a crucial feature for security because it allows us to specify a key that is held in the kernel!

In order to well understand this last sentence, we should go further in this book to the next section; for the moment, let's see some simple usage examples of this tool.

We can use `crypto-afalg` to decrypt data:

```
$ echo "Very secret message" | \
    openssl enc -aes-256-cbc -e \
    -K 0123456789abcdef0123456789abcdef0123456789abcdef01234567
    89abcdef \
    -iv 0123456789abcdef0123456789abcdef > /tmp/secret.enc
$ hexdump -v /tmp/secret.enc
0000000 a1e7 1fa6 ad8c 1825 c4ba 599d 7629 f3f2
0000010 fa9f f0f0 4c73 5f35 8fe4 d5ac 7b3f 9960
0000020
$ cat /tmp/secret.enc | crypto-afalg \
    -K 0123456789abcdef0123456789abcdef0123456789abcdef0123456
    789abcdef \
    -V 0123456789abcdef0123456789abcdef decrypt aes-256-cbc
Very secret message
```

Or we can use it to hash a file:

```
$ echo "My name is Rodolfo Giometti" > /tmp/id.txt
$ openssl dgst -sha256 < /tmp/id.txt
SHA2-256(stdin)= 5e2ea0c72053ce80c13549b2c6e3365098d5bc61015b
39908c78709
0f70189d9
$ crypto-afalg hash sha-256 < /tmp/id.txt
5e2ea0c72053ce80c13549b2c6e3365098d5bc61015b39908c787090f70189d9
```

The tool is (mostly) compatible with the openssl command output data, and it is designed to use the Linux crypto API to do all cryptographic operations and the Linux keyring to manage the keys.

In the case we get the following error:

```
crypto-afalg: socket(AF_ALG): Address family not supported by protocol
```

we should check if the following kernel configuration settings are enabled:

```
CONFIG_CRYPTO_USER=y
CONFIG_CRYPTO_USER_API=y
CONFIG_CRYPTO_USER_API_HASH=y
CONFIG_CRYPTO_USER_API_SKCIPHER=y
```

Before closing this section, recall what we have found above within the /proc/crypto file:

```
name            : tk(cbc(aes))
driver          : tk-cbc-aes-caam
...
min keysize   : 36
max keysize   : 164
ivsize        : 16
...
```

While for the second one we have the values:

```
name            : cbc(aes)
driver          : cbc-aes-caam
...
min keysize   : 16
```

```
max keysize  : 32
ivsize       : 16
...
```

The reader should notice in the above output that we have two different AES-ECB implementations supported by the CAAM (the **Cryptographic Acceleration and Assurance Module** found on many NXP i.MX-based devices): one named `ecb(aes)` and the other named `tk(ecb(aes))`.

What is crucial here is that we have the same AES-CBC algorithm, but it works on different keys! What the word *different* means here will be clearer later when we are going to do some examples; now the reader should keep in mind this interesting difference that is not present in OpenSSL.

1.3 The Linux Key-Management Facility

The **Linux Key-Management Facility**, also known as the **Linux Kernel Key Retention Service** or **Linux Keyring**, is a core component of Linux that is primarily a way for various kernel components to retain or cache security data, authentication keys, encryption keys, and other data in the kernel.

As reported in the keyrings manpages (`man 7 keyrings`), system calls, a library, and some user-space utilities are provided to allow access to the facility:

```
KEYRINGS(7)                 Linux Programmer's Manual
          KEYRINGS(7)

NAME
      keyrings - in-kernel key management and retention
      facility
```

DESCRIPTION

The Linux key-management facility is primarily a way
for various kernel components to retain or cache
security data, authentication keys, encryption keys, and
other data in the kernel.

System call interfaces are provided so that user-space
programs can manage those objects and also use the
facility for their own purposes; see add_key(2),
request_key(2), and keyctl(2).

A library and some user-space utilities are provided
to allow access to the facility. See keyctl(1),
keyctl(3), and keyutils(7) for more information.

...

All these tools can be used in several ways and to solve several
problems, but from our perspective, their primary purpose is to allow user-space programs to store, retrieve, and use cryptographic keys in a secure
and controlled manner.

Curious readers may take a look within kernel documentation in the
Documentation/security/keys directory, or on the Internet at
https://docs.kernel.org/security/keys/).

As reported in the man pages above, one of the most important
commands to manage Linux's keys is keyctl, which has a lot of
subcommands:

```
# keyctl
Format:
  keyctl --version
  keyctl add [-x] <type> <desc> <data> <keyring>
```

```
keyctl chgrp <key> <gid>
keyctl chown <key> <uid>
keyctl clear <keyring>
keyctl describe <keyring>
...
keyctl padd [-x] <type> <desc> <keyring>
...
keyctl read <key>
...
```

For example, the subcommands add and padd are used to add a new key of the specified type and description <desc>. The key is instantiated with the given data and attached to the specified *keyring*.

In this book, what a *keyring* is not explained in detail; however, we can say that it is merely a special key that contains a list of other keys that can be addressed by different entities, just the same as directories and files!

With the keyctl command, we can use the @u and @s (and other) special descriptors to refer to specific keyrings: by using @u, we address the *user keyring*, while by using @s, we address the *session keyring*.

In the Linux keyring system, these special identifiers are used by command line tools like keyctl to refer to specific, predefined keyrings without needing to know their serial numbers (remember that a keyring is just a key holding other keys).

The **session keyring** is tied to a user's login session, so it is created when we log in and is typically destroyed when we log out. It's designed for keys that need to be available for the duration of a user's session (i.e., temporary authentication tokens or keys used by applications launched during that session), and it is inherited by all processes forked from the login shell, making it a convenient place for a single session.

On the other hand, the **user keyring** is a more permanent store of keys; in fact, it is associated with a specific user ID (UID) and persists as long as this ID is active in the kernel. This means it can outlive an individual login session. This keyring is intended for long-term keys that should be available to any process running as that user across different login sessions. For example, a key used by a background service or a `cron` job would be a suitable candidate for the user keyring.

Readers can think of the session keyring (@s) as their wallet for a single day, while the user keyring (@u) is more like a permanent safety deposit box for a specific r.

In the next sections, as soon as we are going to use a new `keyctl` command, everything will become clearer.

Now it's time to take a look at some different key types we can use in our Linux-based system. We will present standard keys (the ones generated via `keyctl`) and non-standard keys that, even if they are vendor-specific, allow obtaining a very high security level (that's why they are presented here).

1.3.1 Plain Text Keys

This kind of key is named *plain text* because it is held within the kernel in a plain text (i.e., in an unencrypted form). This is to differentiate them from the next key types, which are encrypted (or sealed) instead. However, this is just a convention of this book; in the kernel documentation, they are just named as *user* and *logon* keys.

The User Key

The **user** key type has a description and a payload that are arbitrary blobs of data. These can be created, updated, and read by user-space applications and aren't intended for use by kernel services. In fact, as reported in the manpages (`man 7 keyrings`), we have:

```
"user"   This is a general-purpose key type. The key is
         kept entirely within kernel memory. The payload
         may be read and updated by user-space applications.

         The payload for keys of this type is a blob of
         arbitrary data of up to 32,767 bytes.

         The description may be any valid string, though it is
         preferred that it start with a colon-delimited prefix
         representing the service to which the key is of
         interest (for instance "afs:mykey").
```

So, to add a new user key named `userkey` in the user keyring with specified data, we can do as follows:

```
$ keyctl add user userkey "key_data" @u
311176563
```

The `padd` variant of the command reads the data from stdin rather than taking it from the command line, but the two commands are equivalent:

```
$ echo -n "key_data" | keyctl padd user userkey @u
311176563
```

To list all keys in a keyring, we can use the `list` subcommand, as shown below regarding the user keyring:

```
$ keyctl list @u
1 key in keyring:
311176563: --alswrv  1000  1000 user: userkey
```

While to see all keys (and keyrings) we can get access to, we can use the show subcommand:

```
$ keyctl show
Session Keyring
 886145736 --alswrv   1000  1000  keyring: _ses
 821465338 --alswrv   1000 65534   \_ keyring: _uid.1000
 311176563 --alswrv   1000  1000      \_ user: userkey
```

In the first column is the key's serial number (the unique number assigned by the kernel to identify the key), while the last two columns are the **key type** (user) and its name or **description** (userkey). The two numbers 1000 are the **UID** (User ID) and **GID** (Group ID) of the key's owner (for the keyring _uid.1000 the group ID is 65534). In this case, both are 1000, which is the user:

```
$ id -nu 1000
giometti
```

Finally, the string --alswrv identifies the permissions granted to the key. Each letter represents a specific operation:

- a (alter): It grants permission to change the key's attributes, such as its expiration time or permissions. This is considered an administrative permission.

- l (link): It grants permission to create a link from another keyring to this key.

- s (search): It grants permissions to find the key when searching a keyring. Without this, a user might not even be able to locate the key.

- w (write): It grants permission to change or update the key's payload (the actual data in the key).

- r (read): It grants permission to read the key's payload.

- v (view): This is the most basic permission, and it grants permission to view the key's metadata, such as its type and description.

All these permissions are referred to the user that created the key; however, similarly to UNIX file permissions, we have other entities that can access a key: the group, the other, and the possessor. These permissions can be viewed by using the describe subcommand:

```
$ keyctl describe 311176563
311176563: alswrv-----v------------  1000  1000 user: userkey
```

The alswrv string is repeated four times to specify, respectively, *possessor*, *user*, *group*, and *others* permissions. So, in the above example, the *possessor* has full access, while the user has *view* only, while the group and others have no access at all.

While the concept of *user*, *group*, and *other* can be something known by every UNIX user, the concept of *possessor* is something exotic and specific to the Linux key management system. It is a kernel-level access control mechanism, and it is not a user-level attribute we can query directly.

The scope of this book is not to explain in detail this mechanism, and curious readers can get further information in the file Documentation/security/keys/core.rst in the Linux sources, but for the sake of completeness, we can say that the possessor is such a process that has a searchable link to the key from one of its keyrings.

Just to give an example of this fact, we can consider this case under Yocto Scarthgap:

```
# echo -n "key_data" | keyctl padd user userkey @u
827367125
```

The key userkey has been created within the user keyring, but when we try to read back the key's payload, we get the following error:

```
# keyctl pipe 827367125
keyctl_read_alloc: Required key not available
```

This is because we are not the possessor of the key! In fact, if we use the show subcommand (that, by default, recursively shows what keyrings a process is subscribed to and what keys and keyrings they contain), we get the following output:

```
# keyctl show
Session Keyring
 266575291 --alswrv      0      0  keyring: _ses
 823416424 ----s-rv      0      0  \_ user: invocation_id
```

The key is not here; it is in the user keyring:

```
# keyctl show @u
Keyring
1008686124 --alswrv      0 65534  keyring: _uid.0
 827367125 --alswrv      0      0  \_ user: userkey
```

And the only way to get access to it is to link the user keyring to the session keyring as shown below:

```
# keyctl link @u @s
# keyctl show
Session Keyring
 266575291 --alswrv      0      0  keyring: _ses
```

```
 823416424 ----s-rv        0     0   \_ user: invocation_id
1008686124 --alswrv        0 65534   \_ keyring: _uid.0
 827367125 --alswrv        0     0     \_ user: userkey
```

Now we are the possessor of the key, and we can get back its payload:

```
# keyctl pipe 827367125
key_data
```

The act of linking the @u and @s keyrings is a trick widely used in this book, and it will be clearer later when we are going to real usage examples.

The Logon Key

A **logon**, as the user key type, has a payload that is an arbitrary blob of data, but, on the other side, it is intended as a place to store secrets that are accessible to the kernel space only! From the user space perspective, these are write-only keys, so user-space programs cannot read them back anymore.

Another difference between a *logon* key and a *user* key is that the description can be arbitrary but must be prefixed with a non-zero length string that describes the key subclass. The subclass is separated from the rest of the description by a colon (:) character.

Note that the inclusion of a prefix for the user key type is recommended but is not enforced.

In fact, if we try to create a new logon key, we get an error as shown below:

```
$ echo -n "key_data" | keyctl padd logon logonkey @u
add_key: Invalid argument
```

The correct command is:

```
$ echo -n "key_data" | keyctl padd logon logonkey: @u
779318636
```

Or:

```
$ echo -n "key_data" | keyctl padd logon logonkey:testing @u
676851583
```

If we take a look at our user keyring, we should get the following output:

```
$ keyctl list @u
3 keys in keyring:
447352331: --alswrv  1000  1000 user: userkey
676851583: --alsw-v  1000  1000 logon: logonkey:testing
779318636: --alsw-v  1000  1000 logon: logonkey:
```

Now, for example, if we try to read the key named logonkey:, we should get the following result:

```
$ keyctl pipe 779318636
keyctl_read_alloc: Operation not supported
```

Note that this is not just because we have the read permission flag (r); in fact, if we try to add it with the setperm subcommand:

```
$ keyctl setperm 779318636 0x003f0000
$ keyctl list @u
3 keys in keyring:
447352331: --alswrv  1000  1000 user: userkey
676851583: --alsw-v  1000  1000 logon: logonkey:testing
779318636: --alswrv  1000  1000 logon: logonkey:
```

The final result is still the same:

```
$ keyctl pipe 779318636
keyctl_read_alloc: Operation not supported
```

To better understand the key permission flags (and their hexadecimal representation), we can also take a look at the `keyctl` manpages (`man 1 keyctl`) in the section about the `setperm` subcommand, as shown below:

Set the permissions mask on a key

```
keyctl setperm <key> <mask>
```

This command changes the permission control mask on a key. The mask may be specified as a hex number if it begins "0x", an octal number if it begins "0" or a decimal number otherwise.

The hex numbers are a combination of:

```
Possessor   UID       GID        Other      Permission  Granted

========    =======   ========   ========   ====
01000000    00010000  00000100   00000001   View
02000000    00020000  00000200   00000002   Read
04000000    00040000  00000400   00000004   Write
08000000    00080000  00000800   00000008   Search
10000000    00100000  00001000   00000010   Link
20000000    00200000  00002000   00000020   Set Attribute
3f000000    003f0000  00003f00   0000003f   All
```

View permits the type, description and other parameters of a key to be viewed.

Read permits the payload (or keyring list) to be read if supported by the type.

Write permits the payload (or keyring list) to be modified or updated.

Search on a key permits it to be found when a keyring to which it is linked is searched.

Link permits a key to be linked to a keyring.

Now, to give a simple example about how we can use logon keys in a very useful manner regarding security, we can try to decrypt our very secret message just encrypted in the previous section.

First, we must translate the encryption key from a string to binary data; to do so, we can use the following simple program:

```
$ printf "$(echo 0123456789abcdef0123456789abcdef0123456789abcd
ef0123456
789
abcdef | sed 's/\(..\)/\\x\1/g')" > /tmp/key.bin
$ hexdump -v /tmp/key.bin
0000000 2301 6745 ab89 efcd 2301 6745 ab89 efcd
0000010 2301 6745 ab89 efcd 2301 6745 ab89 efcd
0000020
```

Another way to do the above is by using the xxd command as shown below:

```
$ echo 0123456789abcdef0123456789abcdef0123456
789abcdef0123456789abcdef | \
    xxd -r -p > /tmp/key.bin
$ hexdump -v /tmp/key.bin

0000000 2301 6745 ab89 efcd 2301 6745 ab89 efcd
```

```
0000010 2301 6745 ab89 efcd 2301 6745 ab89 efcd
0000020
```

However, the `xxd` command is available on every system; that's why we have used the `print`/`sed` commands, which are quite always present indeed.

Now we put our encryption key within a logon key:

```
$ keyctl padd logon cypher: @s < /tmp/key.bin
591970105
```

From this point until the system reboot, the key is available from the kernel only! However, as seen in the above section "The Linux Crypto API," we can ask the kernel to use it for us via the `crypto-afal` program, which uses the crypto API interface, as shown below:

```
$ cat /tmp/secret.enc | crypto-afalg decrypt aes-256-cbc \
    -S 591970105 -V 0123456789abcdef0123456789abcdef
Very secret message
```

Note that the `crypto-afalg` command also supports the possibility to specify the key's name instead of its serial number:

```
$ cat /tmp/secret.enc | crypto-afalg decrypt aes-256-cbc \
    -S @s,logon,cypher: -V 0123456789abcdef0123456789abcdef
Very secret message
```

Note also that this switch is available only if `ALG_SET_KEY_BY_KEY_SERIAL` is defined, which requires at least a kernel version 6.2.

This last way of operation is more secure because, if we define the logon key in a secure environment (and we will see what we are talking about in the section "A/B Schema" in Chapter 3), the next encryption and decryption operations don't need to specify the key in the command line or from the filesystem anymore!

1.3.2 Sealed Keys

By using the term *sealed*, we mean such keys that are created in the kernel, and user space sees, stores, and loads only encrypted blobs. Regarding the plain text keys seen above, for these keys all user-level blobs are displayed and loaded in hex ASCII for convenience and are integrity verified, giving the system security a great improvement!

Furthermore, these keys are persistent across reboots, unlike the logon keys, which vanish on a reboot (this last feature will be clearer later in "The Linux Transparent Encryption" section).

The Trusted Key

Trusted keys are called in this manner (a.k.a. *trusted*) because they require the availability of a **trusted source** (see below) to be generated and wrapped for greater security.

Both trusted and encrypted keys are stored in the kernel in an encrypted form. However, for trusted keys, the sealing process relies on a trusted source, while for encrypted keys, the sealing process relies on a trusted key (also referred to as the *master key*).

Another (minor) difference between these two key types is that trusted keys are random numbers, while the encrypted keys can be random or user-defined numbers, and since encrypted keys do not depend on a trust source for the seal/unseal step, they are usually faster when used for encryption/decryption.

At the time of the writing of this book, available trusted sources are

- *TPM*: Keys are generated within the **Trusted Platform Module**. It is a specialized chip designed to enhance security by securely storing cryptographic keys, so the strength of random numbers may vary from one device manufacturer to another.

- *TEE or OP-TEE*: The **Open Portable Trusted Execution Environment** is an open source Trusted Execution Environment (TEE) based on Arm TrustZone technology. The random numbers can be hardware or software generated, and they can be seeded via multiple entropy sources.

- *CAAM*: The **Cryptographic Acceleration and Assurance Module** (included in many i.MX CPUs from NXP) is cryptographic acceleration hardware that implements block encryption, hashing and authentication algorithms, a secure memory controller, and a hardware random number generator that can be used to create our trusted key.

Note that the module also implements specific hardware-backed cryptographic keys, which can be called *CAAM keys*. This hardware is the basic engine for the secure keys presented in the next section.

- *DCP*: The Data Co-Processor is a crypto accelerator of various i.MX SoCs; this hardware device itself does not provide a dedicated RNG interface, so the kernel default RNG is used.

These sources must be enabled in the kernel configuration via the entries:

```
CONFIG_TRUSTED_KEYS_TPM
CONFIG_TRUSTED_KEYS_TEE
CONFIG_TRUSTED_KEYS_CAAM
CONFIG_TRUSTED_KEYS_DCP
```

The kernel selects the first available device, or we may override this by specifying `trusted.source=tpm` for TPM, `trusted.source=tee` for OP-TEE, etc.

Each crypto device has its own RNG (Random Number Generator) and then trusted keys are generated by using such devices; however, by specifying `trusted.rng=kernel` in the kernel command line, we can override the used RNG with the kernel's random number pool.

To create a trusted key (often called KMK which stands for *Kernel Master Key* or simply *Master Key*), we can use the following command:

```
$  add trusted trustedkey "new 32" @s
837965936
$ keyctl show
Session Keyring
  881546418 --alswrv      0      0  keyring: _ses
  340681727 ----s-rv      0      0   \_ user: invocation_id
  837965936 --alswrv      0      0   \_ trusted: trustedkey
```

In the case the trusted source is TPM, the creation command changes a bit, and it must be expressed as reported below:

```
$ keyctl add trusted tpmtrustedkey \
            "new 32 keyhandle=<handle> keyauth=
            <auth_val>" @s
```

where keyhandle is an ASCII hexadecimal value of a persistent key handler, while keyauth is an ASCII hexadecimal value for sealing the key (see the next section for an example with the TPM as a trusted source).

Note that here, the key is added to the session keyring (@s) so that it's available to all kernel services, not just a single user's session; however, if we wish to bind the key to the user, we can use user keyring @u (see the above section when we talked about key possessors and key access).

If we get no error, which means this kind of key can be generated within our system, we can ask the kernel to read the key with the following command:

```
$ keyctl pipe 837965936 > /tmp/trustedkey.blob
```

Now, if we get a look at what has been stored within the file trustedkey.blob, we can see that it is nothing usable as-is, since the trustedkey key has been wrapped:

```
$ cat /tmp/trustedkey.blob
76e128fb1b6feece33d2fd6f20c46612caffea17d59fc97ddefe68c0703e2d
7d531fe5d7
aa9897e60e1d0ad923a7db4eff22999e04b27dc8a7304f6a3bbdbc9ad8af74
20c0fb433f
```

Note that the key is returned as ASCII hexadecimal values and not as binary raw values.

In this special form, the key is obviously not a 32 byte long key; it is a wrapped key, and then it can be restored to its 32 byte form at the kernel level by using the trusted device only.

This special feature allows this key type to define secure keys that can live across reboots. In fact, after the wrapped file has been located on the mass storage, we can safely reboot the system and then retrieve the key for further usage by using the following command:

```
$ keyctl add trusted trustedkey "load $(cat trustedkey.
blob)" @s
193053675
$ keyctl show
Session Keyring
 805257004 --alswrv        0       0  keyring: _ses
 971013422 ----s-rv        0       0  \_ user: invocation_id
 193053675 --alswrv        0       0  \_ trusted: trustedkey
```

Be sure to save the blob data key into a persistent location before doing a reboot! In our example, we moved the file into root's home directory.

Before closing this section, we should keep in mind how a trusted key is generated.

When a new trusted key is created by using the command:

```
$ keyctl add trusted ... new ...
```

In the kernel, random bytes are generated by using the trusted source's random number generator (or via a kernel generator). The key stays in the kernel in an unencrypted form, and it is obfuscated into a blob when the user space uses the command:

```
$ keyctl pipe ...
```

On the other hand, when the user space does the command:

```
$ keyctl add trusted ... load ...
```

The blob is decrypted by using the trusted source again (see Figure 1-1).

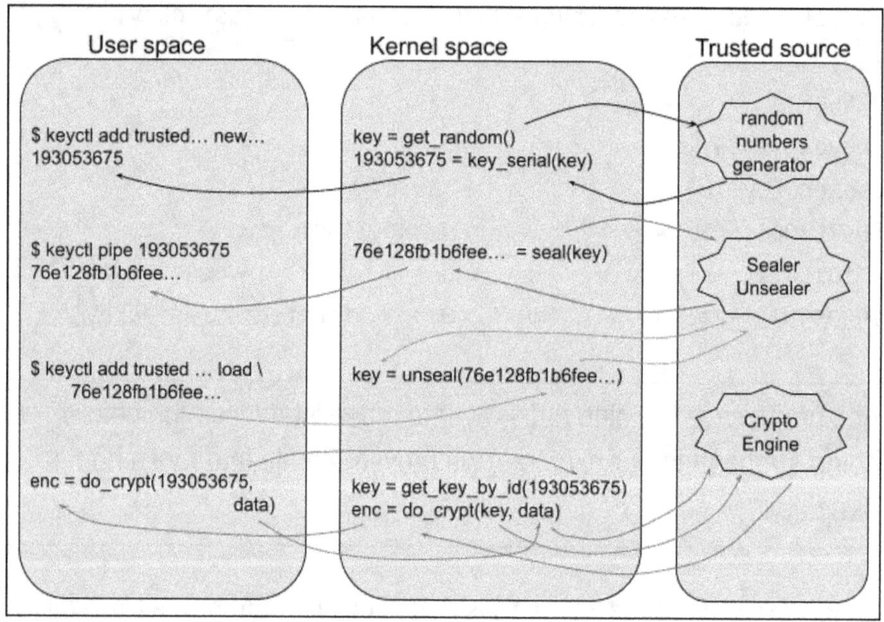

Figure 1-1. *Trusted key management*

In this manner, every trusted key:

- Is not visible outside the kernel

- Its sealed form (visible in user space) is hardware protected

- Is compatible with all crypto engines

The Encrypted Key

Now that we have our trusted key, we can create an **encrypted key**, which is a symmetric key encrypted by the trusted key trustedkey defined above:

```
$ keyctl add encrypted encryptedkey "new
trusted:trustedkey 32" @s
369059404
```

Again, if we try to read the newly created key, a new blob is generated.

```
$ keyctl pipe 369059404 > /tmp/encryptedkey.blob
$ cat /tmp/encryptedkey.blob
default trusted:trustedkey 32
5f389cc214159656f32e169a65faa036007b3fcce4
8d0fbc79d39a157d842ae22ae404a66b591045d1d4cce2a1a25d31f1f2357e
f5f7e995d5
289d90ae2147dbc4bd437752595235812e56e5a1cea52dd0
```

Note that, this time, within the blob there is a clear reference to the master key used to seal the encrypted key. And it's also clear which is the correct procedure to run to restore an encrypted key after a reboot:

```
$ keyctl add trusted trustedkey "load $(cat trustedkey.
blob)" @s
245971746
```

```
$ keyctl add encrypted encryptedkey "load $(cat encryptedkey.
blob)" @s
23711605
```

As a first step, we reload the master key (the trusted key), and then we can reload the encrypted key.

Again, be sure to save the blob data key into a persistent location before issuing a reboot!

At this point the real advantages of these key types are clear if we consider that we can encrypt or decrypt data by using a key that *never* comes in user space! In fact, by using the `crypto-afalg` tool, we can do the following:

```
$ echo "Very secret message" | crypto-afalg encrypt
aes-256-cbc \
                -S @s,encrypted,encryptedkey \
                -V 0123456789abcdef0123456789abcdef > message.enc
$ od -v -t x1 < message.enc
0000000 bb 74 80 53 58 35 1c 66  a6 f6 e3 4a 71 d6 9d 90
0000020 22 57 39 53 11 ab 47 45  e6 68 eb e6 a4 e2 86 3f
0000040
```

Now we can reboot the system, and, to restore the message, we can do as reported below:

```
$ keyctl add trusted trustedkey "load $(cat trustedkey.
blob)" @s
793560228
$ keyctl add encrypted encryptedkey "load $(cat encryptedkey.
blob)" @s
369345434
```

```
$ crypto-afalg decrypt aes-256-cbc \
    -S @s,encrypted,encryptedkey \
    -V 0123456789abcdef0123456789abcdef < message.enc
```

Very secret message

Note that since the trusted keys are hardware related, then the message can only be decrypted on the system that encrypted it!

Encrypted keys are also very useful when used with the eCryptfs filesystem; however, these aspects are covered in this book, and curious readers can get further information in file `Documentation/ security/keys/ecryptfs.rst` within Linux's sources.

Before closing this section, we should spend a few words about a special feature of encrypted keys against the trusted one; that is, the possibility to define them via user-provided decrypted data.

For example, we can define a user-defined key as below:

```
$ userdefkey=$(dd if=/dev/urandom bs=1 count=32 status=none | \
        hexdump -v -e '/1 "%02x"')
$ echo $userdefkey
6bfd52e7c2b6407b9ce67b1c2f9141e41334a9313ab69a280571e92df69df586
$ keyctl add encrypted encuserkey \
            "new default trusted:trustedkey 32 $userdefkey" @s
940228585
```

In the case the command returns the following error:

```
add_key: Invalid argument
```

And in the kernel messages, we see the next warning:

```
trusted_key: encrypted key: instantiation of keys using
provided decrypted data is disabled since CONFIG_USER_
DECRYPTED_DATA is set to false
```

Then we must set in the kernel configuration:

```
CONFIG_USER_DECRYPTED_DATA=y
```

Moreover, note that the `default` format is optional, and it is used by default if omitted. In fact, this command is equivalent to:

```
$ keyctl add encrypted evm "new user:kmk 32 $userdefkey" @s
```

If everything works well, our new encrypted key is created:

```
$ keyctl show
Session Keyring
1050563941 --alswrv        0      0  keyring: _ses
 792764000 ----s-rv        0      0   \_ user: invocation_id
 940228585 --alswrv        0      0   \_ encrypted: encuserkey
 255067523 --alswrv        0      0   \_ trusted: trustedkey
```

If we try to read it, we get the usual sealed data;

```
$ keyctl print 940228585
default trusted:trustedkey 32 c397132ba92477eee9432df1738b6bbc0
02652b157
f9f27bc1c9d81fd227081e17f86d5cbb37e07922aed7cf8a1e2361110c3c75
92640848d0
c2cd94fa5453deea2dc279e366212c9d841e7e378b3962e3
```

But if we use it to do, for example, a decryption, we should get something as shown below:

```
$ echo "Very secret message" | openssl enc -aes-256-cbc -e \
    -K $userdefkey -iv 0123456789abcdef0123456789abcdef \
    > message.enc
```

```
$ hexdump -v message.enc
000000  e7d5 8d4e a444 4c62 dee7 9032 4423 b534
000010  b29c a211 365b c499 4bd1 95e2 c03e ad7a
000020
```

And then decrypt via our just created encrypted key:

```
$ crypto-afalg decrypt aes-256-cbc -S @s,encrypted,encuserkey \
    -V 0123456789abcdef0123456789abcdef < message.enc
Very secret message
```

1.3.3 Vendor-Specific Keys

In the previous section we presented the trusted keys, that is, keys generated within a trusted source that we can use to seal the encrypted keys. However, according to a specific CPU vendor's support for Linux, we can have more key types for different usages.

For example, as seen above, several CPUs of the iMX family have the CAAM, which is a hardware device that can do several crypto activities. NXP provides non-standard tools to allow developers to generate keys by using the CAAM (of course, other CPU vendors can provide similar methods, and what we are going to present here can be adapted to these specific cases with minor effort).

From the NXP's repository at `https://github.com/nxp-imx/keyctl_caam`, we can obtain the `caam-keygen` utility, which allows us to use CAAM to generate keys in a very secure manner. In fact, as already stated before, the CAAM can generate random data and encrypt/decrypt data by itself, so it should be desirable to do all the operations within the CAAM in such a way that the key is generated and sealed/unsealed inside the CAAM itself. Note that this behavior is different from the trusted key one (see "The Trusted Key" section); in fact, in this case the key resides within the CAAM while its sealed form is available in the kernel or user space!

This last concept will be better explained later; for the moment, let's see how we can create and use these special keys.

The caam-keygen usage message is reported below:

```
$ caam-keygen -h
CAAM keygen usage: caam-keygen [options]
Options:
create <key_name> <key_enc> <key_mode> <key_val> <text_type>
        <key_name> the name of the file that will contain the
        black key.
            A file with the same name, but with .bb extension,
            will contain the black blob.
        <key_enc> can be ecb or ccm
        <key_mode> can be -s or -t.
            -s generate a black key from random with the size
                given in the next argument
            -t generate a black key from a plaintext given in
                the next argument
        <key_val> the size or the plaintext based on the previous
        argument (<key_mode>)
        <text_type> can be -h or -p (default argument is -p)
            -h generate a black key from the hex text that is
                provided in previous argument
            -p generate a black key from the plain text that is
                provided in previous argument
import <blob_name> <key_name>
        <blob_name> the absolute path of the file that contains
        the blob
        <key_name> the name of the file that will contain the
        black key.
...
```

So, to create a key, we can use the `create` subcommand, where

- key_name is the name of the file that will contain the key (a file with the same name, but with a `.bb` extension, is also created and will contain the *key blob*. What a key blob is will be explained just below this paragraph).

- key_enc is a string that can be set to `ecb` or `ccm` and it specifies which is the AES algorithm to be used to seal the key (ecb is for AES-ECB and ccm is for AES-CCM. While AES-ECB encryption is intended for quick decryption, AES-CCM encryption is used for high assurance).

- key_mode can be set to `-s` or `-t`, and with the former, a random key is generated with the size given in key_val, while with the latter, a key from a plain text given in key_val is generated instead (so key_val can be the size or the plain text based on the `mode` argument).

- text_type can be `-h` or `-p` (default argument is `-p`) and states the type of the previous argument key_val when we create a key from a plain text. With `-p` we should consider key_val as plain text, while with `-h` we should consider key_val as hexadecimal text (see below for an example).

Firstly, we should underline that these keys are not power-cycle safe. That's why we require the key blob. When we generate a key, the system returns to us the key and the corresponding blob key, which is the method for protecting our key data across system power cycles.

However, it's time to do an example to better understand these concepts. Let's start creating a key from plain text in hexadecimal form:

```
$ caam-keygen create caamkey ecb -t \
    0123456789abcdef0123456789abcdef0123456789abcdef012345678
    9abcdef -h
```

If everything goes well, two new files are created under the /etc/caam directory: the actual key (file caamkey) and the key blob file (caamkey. bb file):

```
$ ls -l /etc/caam/
total 12
-rw-r--r-- 1 root root  52 Mar  5 16:04 caamkey
-rw-r--r-- 1 root root 112 Mar  5 16:04 caamkey.bb
-rw-r--r-- 1 root root  36 Jan  1  1970 rootfs.key
```

Actually, by default, the key files creation is under /data/caam, but our sources have been altered, and this default has been moved to /etc/caam.

As stated above, we need these two files because the caamkey file is the one holding the key we can use until the system is rebooted, while the second is the one we must use across reboots to recover the actual value of the key.

In fact, if we try to use the caamkey file to encrypt or decrypt data after a reboot, we fail! The correct procedure is to regenerate the key from the caamkey.bb file with the subcommand import as shown below:

```
$ caam-keygen import /etc/caam/caamkey.bb caamkey-regen
$ ls -l /etc/caam/
total 16
-rw-r--r-- 1 root root  52 Mar  5 16:04 caamkey
```

```
-rw-r--r-- 1 root root  52 Mar  5 16:06 caamkey-regen
-rw-r--r-- 1 root root 112 Mar  5 16:04 caamkey.bb
-rw-r--r-- 1 root root  36 Jan  1  1970 rootfs.key
```

However, to better explain what we are saying, let's see how we can use our newly created key files. If we recall what we saw in "The Linux Crypto API" section, now it is the case where the `tk(cbc(aes))` crypto algorithm introduced there comes into play with the `crypto-afalg` utility.

Asking to `crypto-afalg` all supported symmetric cipher algorithms, we get the following list:

```
$ crypto-afalg decrypt
crypto-afalg:   name              kernel-name  block(B)  key/iv(B)
crypto-afalg: - aes-128-cbc    cbc(aes)              16    16/16
crypto-afalg: - aes-256-cbc    cbc(aes)              16    32/16
crypto-afalg: - caam(aes-256-cbc)  tk(cbc(aes)) 16    52/16
crypto-afalg:   NOTE: 'x' means 'not available'
```

By specifying the name `caam(aes-256-cbc)`, we ask the tool to use the `tk(cbc(aes))` algorithm, which requires a key 52 bytes long. This is precisely the length of the just created `caamkey` file. In fact, we can encrypt and then decrypt data by doing as shown below:

```
$ keyctl padd user caamkey @s < /etc/caam/caamkey
571751497
```

The above command loads the CAAM key into a user key (note that we can also use a logon key, but since the payload is sealed, even if the key is readable, it is not a problem at all). Then, to do an encryption, we use the command below:

```
$ echo "Very secret message" | \
        crypto-afalg encrypt 'caam(aes-256-cbc)' -S 571751497 \
          -V 0123456789abcdef0123456789abcdef > message.enc
```

```
$ hexdump -v message.enc
0000000 a1e7 1fa6 ad8c 1825 c4ba 599d 7629 f3f2
0000010 fa9f f0f0 4c73 5f35 8fe4 d5ac 7b3f 9960
0000020
```

Note that we have used single quotes to prevent bash expansion for the string `caam(aes-256-cbc)` that has the parentheses. In fact, without a single quote, we will get the error message:

```
-sh: syntax error near unexpected token `('
```

Then to decrypt the message, we can use the inverse operation with OpenSSL:

```
$ openssl enc -d -aes-256-cbc \
    -K 0123456789abcdef0123456789abcdef0123456789abcdef01234567
    89abcdef \
    -iv 0123456789a
bcdef0123456789abcdef < message.enc
Very secret message
```

Another interesting usage of this key, and similar to the one with the trusted keys presented above, is the possibility to generate a random key by using the following command line:

```
$ caam-keygen create caamkey ecb -s 32
```

Now, within the caamkey file, a new 256-bit key is stored, and it is known by the CAAM only! This is a similar situation as per trusted keys; however, there is a crucial difference! While a trusted key is stored in its unsealed form in the kernel, a CAAM key is stored in its unsealed form in the CAAM. When it is moved to the kernel, it is sealed (see Figure 1-2).

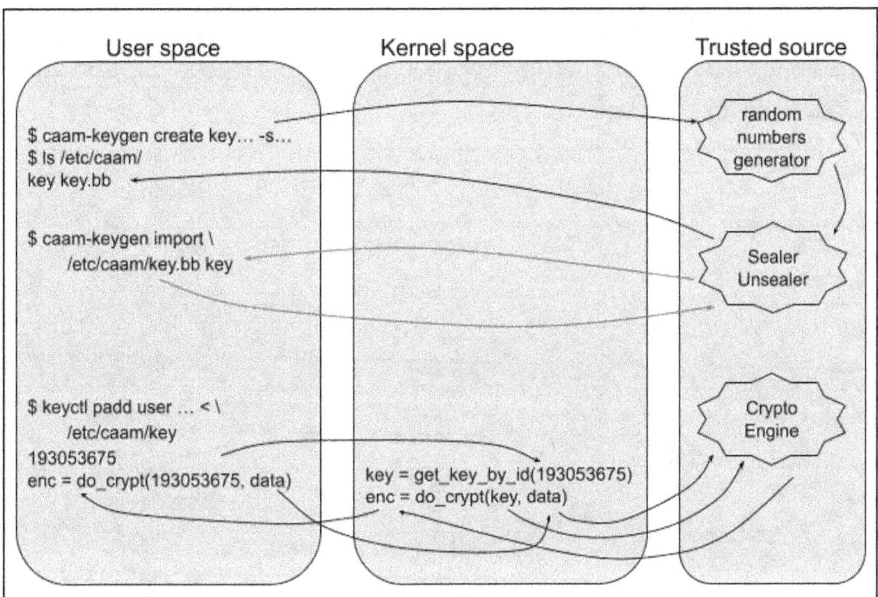

Figure 1-2. *CAAM key management*

Readers should note that in Figures 1-1 and 1-2, the variable key in the kernel doesn't hold the same kind of data; in fact, here it holds a sealed key, while in the case of trusted keys, key holds a key in plain text (even if protected by the kernel).

1.4 The Linux Transparent Encryption

Transparent encryption in Linux refers to a method of protecting data on a storage device with the help of the kernel. In fact, the encryption and decryption happen automatically and on-the-fly. So the data is always encrypted when at rest (on the disk) but appears as plain text to the running operating system and its users when accessed. This approach allows user-space applications to work as if everything were in plain text.

The most common and robust forms of transparent encryption in Linux are based on two different approaches: block-level encryption and filesystem-level encryption.

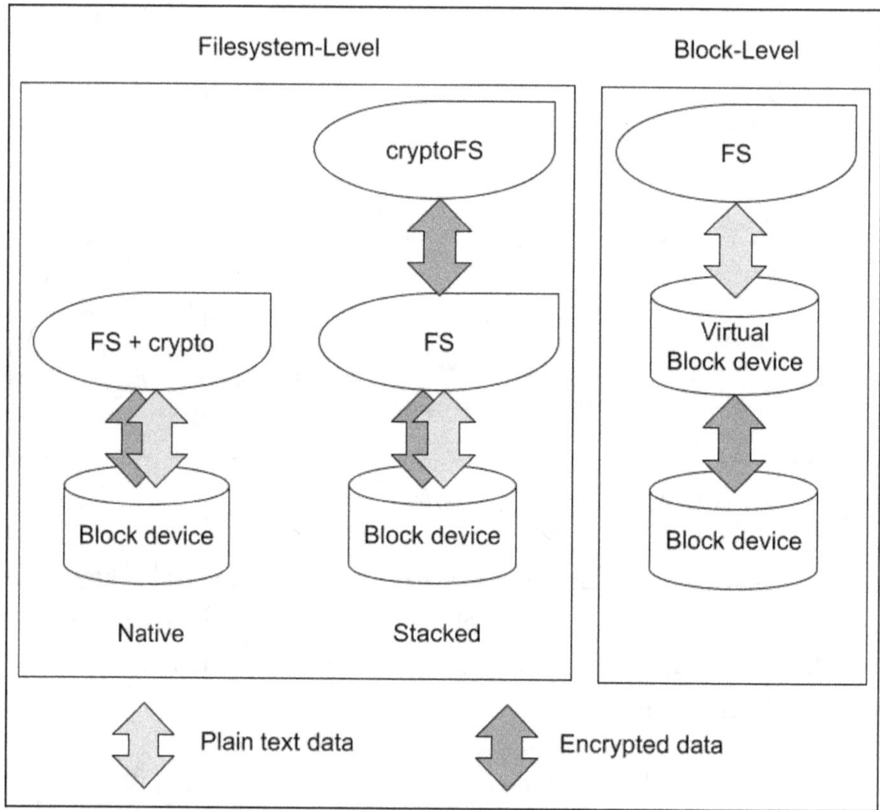

Figure 1-3. *The filesystem-level vs. block-level Linux transparent encryption*

1.4.1 The Filesystem-Level Encryption

The filesystem-level encryption works at a higher level than block-level encryption, and it is designed for more granular control (we mean that it is possible to encrypt some files or directories instead of all files within the filesystem). In a Linux-based system, it can be handled in two ways: as a **stacked filesystem** or as a **native filesystem**.

A stacked encryption filesystem operates on top of an existing filesystem. The upper layer encrypts and decrypts data on the fly as it is written and read from the lower layer filesystem, while the lower layer filesystem sees *normal* files, but their content is encrypted.

On the other hand, native filesystem encryption happens in the filesystem itself, without an upper layer. This means that the filesystem itself has to support encryption; for example, EXT4, F2FS, and UBIFS filesystems support native encryption. This latter approach is currently more popular than the former one, since it's usually more memory-efficient as there is no filesystem stack, and it does not (necessarily) require root permissions for setup. As an example of stacked filesystems, there is eCryptfs, which is a kernel module, or EncFS (`https://github.com/vgough/encfs`) and gocryptfs (`https://github.com/rfjakob/gocryptfs`) both based on FUSE (not covered in this book).

The **Filesystem in Userspace (FUSE)** is a software interface for Linux (and Unix-like systems) that lets non-privileged users create their own filesystems in user space. This is achieved by running filesystem code in user space while the FUSE module provides only a bridge to the actual kernel interfaces.

The eCryptfs is currently not actively developed, so it should not be used in production systems. Other stacked encryption filesystems with FUSE may make sense if our filesystem does not support native encryption or we don't like modifying the kernel.

Using eCryptfs

In order to give a usage example of this filesystem kind, we can consider
the next example with eCryptfs which, even if not suggested for
production, is interesting due to the fact we can use encrypted keys to
secure our files.

First, we must create a master key (that can be a user or trusted key—of
course a trusted key has a higher protection level):

```
$ keyctl add trusted fstkey "new 32" @s | \

        xargs keyctl pipe | tee fstkey.blob
0004b3991ed970df14bd2aca04db02d6ea22ecf7dd0524eb7fde28b0e84a8b5
a16045dde
ff781da6e86cdf4197f77758712656e5252aa32ffb61d1628821272ce3887b9
ab852fdd5
92b242415513fe2c
```

Then we create an encrypted key named abcd100020009900 of length
64 bytes with format ecryptfs and save it using a previously loaded trusted
key fst:

```
$ keyctl add encrypted abcd100020009900 \
        "new ecryptfs trusted:fstkey 64" @s | \
        xargs keyctl pipe | tee fsekey.blob
ecryptfs trusted:fstkey 64 8d41ac6caabda58e275999fd6e0cce
5e00e061d4fa29f
3728b92bb7c9090a2c42daab90bcc6393294e27844c65c4f93d94a429c8054
786e033f62
90b27684feb20e56c56831f19b1e4bdb369bf7c1b07bc625b171d04889155b
297b1d0688c59d5682c3f5ccfae767d8ee1fff1a50335f8
```

Note that the encrypted key name must be composed of 16 hexadecimal characters; if not, the `keyctl add_key` subcommand will fail with the error message:

```
add_key: Invalid argument
```

And within the kernel messages, we should see the following warning:

```
[  110.789884] trusted_key: encrypted_key: key description
must be 16 hexadecimal characters long
```

Now all needed keys should be in place:

```
$ keyctl show
Session Keyring
 350504721 --alswrv       0       0  keyring: _ses
 965075033 ----s-rv       0       0   \_ user: invocation_id
 700290522 --alswrv       0       0   \_ encrypted: abcd100020009900
1012394983 --alswrv       0       0   \_ trusted: fstkey
```

We are ready to mount an eCryptfs filesystem using the created encrypted key abcd100020009900 into the /data/secret directory. To do so, we need the following commands:

```
$ mkdir /data/secret
$ mount -i -t ecryptfs -oecryptfs_sig=abcd100020009900,\
ecryptfs_cipher=aes,ecryptfs_key_bytes=32 \
        /data/secret/ /data/secret/
```

Note that the standard `mount` command syntax requires two paths:

```
# mount -t <type> <device> <mount_point>
```

In the context of eCryptfs, we have a different form (also named *stacked form*):

```
# mount -t ecryptfs <lower_directory> <upper_directory>
```

The `<lower_directory>`, the first instance of `/data/secret/`, acts as the source or the lower directory (the device being mounted). This is the existing directory on the underlying filesystem (Ext4 in our example) that contains the encrypted files. This is where eCryptfs reads and writes the ciphertext. The `<upper_directory>`, the second instance of `/data/secret/`, acts as the target or the mount point (the location where the device is mounted). This is the directory through which we can access the decrypted files.

When the mount is successful, eCryptfs intercepts all access to this path and handles the decryption/encryption on the fly.

In our example, by using the same path for both the lower and upper mount point directories, we are performing an *in-place mount*: that is, before mounting, the encrypted unreadable data; while, after mounting, the decrypted view is layered on top, hiding the raw encrypted files underneath and making the data fully readable and usable.

Now we can use the newly created directory as usual:

```
$ echo 'Very secret data' > /data/secret/message
$ ls -l /data/secret/
total 12
-rw-r--r-- 1 root root 17 Mar  5 16:53 message
$ cat /data/secret/message
Very secret data
```

This is true until we unmount the encrypted filesystem:

```
$ umount /data/secret/
Could not unlink the key(s) from your keying. Please use
`keyctl unlink`
 if you wish to remove the key(s). Proceeding with umount.
```

Now if we try to read within /data/secret the underlying data are exposed:

```
# ls -l /data/secret/
total 12
-rw-r--r-- 1 root root 12288 Mar  5 16:53 message
# hexdump -v /data/secret/message | head
-5
0000000 0000 0000 0000 1100 9fe3 7e65 1edf 8bd2
0000010 0003 0200 0000 0010 0200 2d8c 0904 0103
0000020 0000 0000 0000 0000 8360 fa3b 0c5d 58de
0000030 f62a fc1f bb08 8897 58c1 f0dd 433a c153
0000040 110a 4967 0a82 18b9 edc8 6216 5f08 4f43
```

In the case we do a reboot, to remount the encrypted filesystem to be able to get access to our secrets, we have to (as already shown above):

```
$ keyctl add trusted fstkey \
        "load $(cat fstkey.blob)" @s
```

```
878125141
$ keyctl add encrypted abcd100020009900 \
        "load $(cat fsekey.blob)" @s
330303616
```

And then redo the mount:

```
$ mount -i -t ecryptfs -oecryptfs_sig=abcd100020009900,\
ecryptfs_cipher=aes,ecryptfs_key_bytes=32 \
        /data/secret/ /data/secret/
```

Now all secrets are accessible again:

```
$ cat /data/secret/message
Very secret data
```

For further information about this filesystem, a good starting point is the file `Documentation/security/keys/ecryptfs.rst` within the kernel sources.

Using fscrypt

Regarding the native filesystem-level encryption, we said above that we must use a filesystem that supports this mechanism. One of these filesystem is EXT4, which is one of the most used filesystems, so let's see a simple example with this filesystem.

To manage native filesystem-level encryption, we can use the `fscrypt` tool; its usage message is reported below:

```
$ fscrypt -h
fscrypt: flag: help requested

Usage:
  fscrypt COMMAND [arguments] [options]
```

```
Commands:
  setup      - perform global setup or filesystem setup
  encrypt    - enable filesystem encryption for a directory
  unlock     - unlock an encrypted directory
  lock       - lock an encrypted directory
  purge      - Remove a filesystem's keys
  status     - print the global, filesystem, or file status
  metadata   - [ADVANCED] manipulate the policy or protector
               metadata

Options:
  --verbose          Prints additional debug messages to
                     standard output.

  --quiet            Prints nothing to standard output except
                     for errors. Selects the default for any
                     options that would normally show a prompt.

  --help             Prints help screen for commands and
                     subcommands.

  --version          Prints version information.
```

Before starting our operations, we must execute the `fscrypt setup` command. This command prepares the filesystem for native encryption; in our example, we must do as shown below (for simplicity, we do all commands as root):

```
# fscrypt setup
Defaulting to policy_version 2 because kernel supports it.
Customizing passphrase hashing difficulty for this system...
Created global config file at "/etc/fscrypt.conf".
Allow users other than root to create fscrypt metadata on
the root
```

```
filesystem? (See https://github.com/google/fscrypt#setting-up-
fscrypt-on-a-filesystem) [y/N]
Metadata directories created at "/.fscrypt", writable by
root only.
# fscrypt setup /data/
Allow users other than root to create fscrypt metadata on this
filesystem? (See https://github.com/google/fscrypt#setting-up-
fscrypt-on-a-filesystem) [y/N]
Metadata directories created at "/data/.fscrypt", writable by
root only.
```

The first command is needed to create the global config file at /etc/fscrypt.conf, while the second one is to set up the /data mountpoint.

In the previous example, we pressed the ENTER key for all questions to select the default answer.

Note that we may get the following error message:

```
# fscrypt encrypt /data/
[ERROR] fscrypt encrypt: encryption not enabled on filesystem
                        /data (/dev/mmcblk2p5).
```

To enable encryption support on this filesystem, run as privileged user:

```
# tune2fs -O encrypt "/dev/mmcblk2p5"
```

In this case, fscrypt suggests to us how to recover; however, we should also ensure that the kernel has CONFIG_FS_ENCRYPTION=y, for example, by using the command below, which reads the current kernel configuration settings:

```
# zgrep CONFIG_FS_ENCRYPTION /proc/config.gz
CONFIG_FS_ENCRYPTION=y
```

However, we can use the `fscrypt status` subcommand to see which of the available mount points can be used with the filesystem-level encryption:

```
# fscrypt status
filesystems supporting encryption: 1
filesystems with fscrypt metadata: 2

MOUNTPOINT  DEVICE          FILESYSTEM  ENCRYPTION   FSCRYPT
/           /dev/dm-0       ext4        not enabled  Yes
/boot       /dev/mmcblk2p1  ext4        not enabled  No
/data       /dev/mmcblk2p5  ext4        supported    Yes
/factory    /dev/mmcblk2p2  ext4        not enabled  No
```

If we try to execute `fscrypt setup` on /data, we will get the following error message, which notifies us that the filesystem is already set up:

```
# fscrypt setup /data/
[ERROR] fscrypt setup: filesystem /data is already setup for
                       use with fscrypt
```

Then we can go further by creating our new encrypted directory in /data/secret:

```
# mkdir /data/secret/
# fscrypt encrypt /data/secret/
The following protector sources are available:
1 - Your login passphrase (pam_passphrase)
2 - A custom passphrase (custom_passphrase)
3 - A raw 256-bit key (raw_key)
Enter the source number for the new protector [2 - custom_
passphrase]:
```

```
Enter a name for the new protector: my_passphrase
Enter custom passphrase for protector "my_passphrase":
Confirm passphrase:
"/data/secret/" is now encrypted, unlocked, and ready for use.
```

In the above example, we have used a custom passphrase to protect our secrets, but we can also use a raw key or even our login passphrase.

The fscrypt's most convenient feature is obviously its integration with PAM (the Pluggable Authentication Modules) for automatic unlocking. This allows the system to use our user login password to unlock the encrypted directory as soon as we log in, eliminating the need to enter a second, separate passphrase.

However, this topic is beyond the scope of this book, so we'll leave it to the reader to see how to enable this feature.

Now we can put all secret files within our directory, and we can verify that everything works as normal:

```
# echo 'Very secret data' > /data/secret/message
[ 1188.343167] fscrypt: AES-256-CTS-CBC using implementation
"cts-cbc-aes-ce"
[ 1188.350141] fscrypt: AES-256-XTS using implementation
"xts-aes-ce"
# ls -l /data/secret/
total 4
-rw-r--r-- 1 root root 17 Mar  5 15:33 message
# cat /data/secret/message
Very secret data
```

By using the `status` subcommand, we can also check our directory's status and information:

```
# fscrypt status /data/secret/
"/data/secret/" is encrypted with fscrypt.

Policy:    210a162753f56ed370168972fd0e2892
Options:   padding:32 contents:AES_256_XTS filenames:AES_256_CTS
           policy_version:2
Unlocked: Yes

Protected with 1 protector:
PROTECTOR          LINKED  DESCRIPTION
3339aec226ce34fe   No       custom protector "my_passphrase"
```

Once we have finished, we wish to lock and protect our secrets; we can use the `lock` subcommand to inform the kernel that the data must be locked.

```
# fscrypt lock /data/secret/
"/data/secret/" is now locked.
```

Starting from this point, all data are locked, and we can verify it by trying to inspect the /data/secret directory again:

```
# ls -l /data/secret/
total 4
-rw-r--r-- 1 root root 17 Mar  5 15:33 PplT7iszahTMmVzke6Pmn
dUPMsvJL1mNeFWAh9XgAXyStEJqEO3jOQ
# hexdump -v /data/secret/PplT7iszahTMmVzke6PmndUPMsvJL1mNe
FWAh9XgAXyStEJqEO3jOQ
hexdump: /data/secret/PplT7iszahTMmVzke6PmndUPMsvJL1mNe
FWAh9XgAXyStEJqEO
3jOQ: Required key not available
hexdump: all input file arguments failed
```

As we can see in the above output, not only are all files encrypted, but also, if we try to read their content, we get an error!

To unlock our /data/secret directory again, or after a reboot, we must use the unlock subcommand and reenter our passphrase:

```
# fscrypt unlock /data/secret/
Enter custom passphrase for protector "my_passphrase":
"/data/secret/" is now unlocked and ready for use.
# cat /data/secret/message
Very secret data
```

In the above example, we didn't use the Linux keyring as in previous examples to manage the encryption keys; this is because the fscrypt tool doesn't provide an interface to do that directly. More precisely, fscrypt uses the *filesystem-level keyrings* to do its job. In fact, filesystem-level keyrings were introduced specifically to handle fscrypt native encryption; instead of being a general-purpose database, this is a specialized API (based on the ioctl command FS_IOC_ADD_ENCRYPTION_KEY—see file include/uapi/linux/fscrypt.h in the Linux sources) that links a key directly to a specific disk partition.

The filesystem-level keyrings and related topics are not covered in this book since, even if very interesting for the system security in general, they have very low impact on the Secure Boot.

For the sake of completeness, we briefly report a legacy way to use an encryption key to encrypt a directory. Readers that wish to use it in their system should be aware that this trick must be used carefully, or they may experience drawbacks!

To use the Linux keyring, we can use the FS_IOC_SET_ENCRYPTION_POLICY and FS_IOC_GET_ENCRYPTION_POLICY commands (located in the same file

of FS_IOC_ADD_ENCRYPTION_KEY) as done in the little program fscrypt_
v1(downloadable from https://github.com/giometti/fscrypt_v1).

Once downloaded and compiled (easy tasks left to the readers), we can use it as shown in the usage message:

```
$ fscrypt_v1
usage: fscrypt_v1 <dir>
```

The directory to be encrypted should be within a filesystem that supports the encryption as per the above fscrypt example, so we can use the new directory /data/secret_v1 as shown below:

```
$ mkdir /data/secret_v1
```

Now we must create our key:

```
$ dd if=/dev/urandom bs=64 count=1 > fscryptkey.data
```

Then we can do the encryption by passing the key to the fscrypt_v1 tool through the stdin stream:

```
$ fscrypt_v1 /data/secret_v1 < fscryptkey.data
Policy v1 successfully applied to /data/secret_v1 with key
'fscrypt:3c08
d8d67ccccc1f' (ID: 910697476) successfully added to
session keyring
```

Note that we execute the tool the kernel says:

```
[ 2076.776746] fscrypt_v1 (pid 800) is setting deprecated v1
encryption
policy; recommend upgrading to v2.
```

This is because, as already said, this mode of operation is legacy, and it should not be used in a production environment!

Now a new logon key named `fscrypt:3c08d8d67ccccc1f` should be added to our session keyring:

```
$ keyctl show
Session Keyring
 967757655 --alswrv        0      0  keyring: _ses
 481010371 ----s-rv        0      0  \_ user: invocation_id
 910697476 --alsw-v        0      0  \_ logon:
                                         fscrypt:3c08d8d67ccccc1f
```

Perfect! Now everything is up and running, and we can start adding new secret files:

```
$ echo "secret message" > /data/secret_v1/message
$ ls /data/secret_v1/
message
$ cat /data/secret_v1/message
secret message
```

Note that, even in this case, the kernel prints similar information to above, where we used the new fscrypt policy:

```
[ 2623.893635] fscrypt: AES-256-CTS-CBC using implementation
"cts-cbc-aes-ce"
[ 2623.900690] fscrypt: AES-256-XTS using implementation
"xts-aes-ce"
```

Now, to verify that the file is inaccessible when the encryption is disabled, we must remove the logon key and flush the cache as shown below:

```
$ keyctl unlink 910697476 @s
$ sync && echo 3 > /proc/sys/vm/drop_caches
```

Here we can see one of the reasons why this approach has been
replaced. Simply speaking, even after we tell keyring to remove a
key, the filesystem doesn't just forget the data because the Linux
kernel is designed to be as fast as possible by caching everything in
RAM. And the two last commands are the *gold standard* for ensuring
an encrypted directory is truly locked and inaccessible.

At this point, if we try to read the data, we cannot:

```
$ ls /data/secret_v1/
IKENUQoj8qIDnLDZKCYHqOONALqsp2n5dwo9kQB4IOmyXu48ScZfng
```

To get access again to our secrets, we must reexecute the `fscrypt_v1`
tool as above.

1.4.2 The Block-Level Encryption

The **block-level encryption**, instead, works at a lower level, that is, at the
block device level, and it is used to get a transparent disk encryption on
Linux. Once an encrypted (and virtual) block device is generated, we can
place a filesystem on it as we do for a normal block device (see Figure 1-3).

Just to give an idea about what we are talking about, we report below
the commands needed to create this kind of block device.

Firstly, we must generate a key:

```
$ openssl rand 32 > blockdev.key
$ BLOCKDEV_KEYHEX=$(cat blockdev.key | hexdump -v -e '/1 "%02x"')
$ echo $BLOCKDEV_KEYHEX
eb03925f0f31b70ecce1f220a26d33dfee1e8ccccdc0832b81176b158f530cab
```

Then we need a real block device to encrypt. We can use a USB key, or any available disk, or a single partition of them; however, since we have no sacrificial devices, we decide to use a loop device.

A **loop device** (or *loopback* device) in Linux is a pseudo-block device that allows a regular file to be treated as if it were a physical storage device (like a hard drive or a partition). It is a kernel abstraction that essentially makes a loop back from the filesystem layer to the data contained within the file.

A good starting point to get further information on these devices and their usage is the manpages man 4 loop.

So, let's create an empty file:

```
$ dd if=/dev/zero of=blockdev.bin bs=1M count=16
```

And then connect a loop device to it by using the losetup command:

```
$ BLOCKDEV=$(losetup -f --show blockdev.bin)
[12041.483652] loop0: detected capacity change from 0 to 32768
$ echo $BLOCKDEV
/dev/loop0
```

Great! Now we can use the newly created block device /dev/loop0!

Two notes:

1)   Starting from this point, some commands may require root privileges, depending on the reader system settings. It is up to the reader to decide whether to give them root user or use the command sudo.

2)   The loop device can have a different name; for example, /dev/loop1, /dev/loop37, etc. It's a normal behavior.

Now we require some information regarding the block device, especially we need to know the total disk length in 512-byte sectors. To do so, we can use the blockdev command as reported below:

```
$ SECTORS=$(blockdev --getsz /dev/loop0)
$ echo $SECTORS
32768
```

Now we can define our encrypted device by using the dmsetup command:

```
$ dmsetup create cryptdev --table \
    "0 $SECTORS crypt aes-cbc-plain $BLOCKDEV_KEYHEX 0
    $BLOCKDEV 0"
```

The above command creates the cryptdev device by using the parameters specified in the table (the argument of --table); each argument, in order as they appear, means

- 0: The starting sector where the encryption begins.

- $SECTORS: As already stated above, the total disk length in 512-byte sectors.

- crypt: The target type of the command line. In our case it is fixed to crypt, which means cryptography via dm-crypt.

- aes-cbc-plain: This is a composed string; that is, -plain is a postfix that specifies as initial vectors (IV) the 32-bit little-endian version of the sector number, padded with zeros if necessary. This is a way to have different encryption for sectors holding the same data and to speed up the encryption/decryption operations. This is because the system doesn't need to read the vectors from the metadata stored somewhere on the disk.

Stated this, `aes-cbc` is the real kernel name of the encryption algorithm to be used.

- $BLOCKDEV_KEYHEX: This is our encryption key.

- 0: The offset in sectors where the initial vectors are stored or where the parameters needed to generate the initial vectors reside. Since we are using `-plain`, it must be set to 0.

- $BLOCKDEV: The name of the block device to encrypt (i.e., the mapped device).

- 0: Starting offset on the mapped device.

Other optional parameters can follow, but they are out of the scope of this book. Curious readers can take a look at the `dmsetup` manpages (`man 8 dmsetup`).

If everything works well, we should get no errors, and a new entry should appear under the directory /dev/mapper, as reported below:

```
$ ls /dev/mapper/
control  cryptdev  root
```

The root is an already present mapped device within our system, while control is a character device used by dmsetp and friends to communicate with the kernel to manage all mapped devices.

On most systems these files are automatically created by udev; however, below in this section we are going to show how to create these devices by hand.

OK, the newly created block device /dev/mapper/cryptdev can now be formatted as usual:

```
$ mkfs.ext4 /dev/mapper/cryptdev
mke2fs 1.47.0 (5-Feb-2023)
Creating filesystem with 16384 1k blocks and 4096 inodes
Filesystem UUID: 587b0cc6-74a9-49eb-af2e-be350bc7bc6f
Superblock backups stored on blocks:
        8193

Allocating group tables: done
Writing inode tables: done
Creating journal (1024 blocks): done
Writing superblocks and filesystem accounting information: done
```

And then mounted:

```
$ mount /dev/mapper/cryptdev /mnt/
[12649.467885] EXT4-fs (dm-1): mounted filesystem
587b0cc6-74a9-49eb-af2
e-be350bc7bc6f r/w with ordered data mode. Quota mode: none.
```

We can also add a text file:

```
$ echo 'Very secret data' > /mnt/file
$ ls /mnt/
file  lost+found
```

```
$ cat /mnt/file
Very secret data
```

Everything works as usual, but the difference is that whatever is written in /dev/mapper/cryptdev is encrypted on the fly and then saved into /dev/loop0, and vice versa, whatever we try to read in /dev/mapper/cryptdev is first read in /dev/loop0 and then decrypted on the fly.

To verify it, we can try to see what the kernel has saved into the two devices. So, let's unmount /dev/mapper/cryptdev to be certain it is correctly closed:

```
$ umount /mnt/
[12684.146255] EXT4-fs (dm-1): unmounting filesystem
587b0cc6-74a9-49eb-af2e-be350bc7bc6f.
```

Then let's attempt to detect where the string Very secret data has been saved into the /dev/mapper/cryptdev device:

```
$ hexdump -Cv /dev/mapper/cryptdev
...
00980400  56 65 72 79 20 73 65 63  72 65 74 20 64 61 74
61  |Very secret data|
...
```

Since this is the plain text device, we can easily find our data. On the other hand, in the /dev/loop0 device, the corresponding sector is encrypted! In fact, we have the following:

```
$ hexdump -C /dev/loop0
...
009803f0  00 00 00 00 00 00 00 00  00 00 00 00 00 00 00 00
|................|
00980400  88 57 4c 87 b5 2d 05 ac  96 0b 8f 70 a2 79 3f cd
|.WL..-.....p.y?.|
```

```
00980410  14 43 da 27 6a ad fc 6b  5a 84 1a fc 87 42 cc c6
|.C.'j..kZ....B..|
...
```

This is really fascinating, but an attentive reader will have noticed that the above example has a security problem: the encryption key is readable! To solve this issue, we can use a trusted (or encrypted) key, as shown in the next section.

Using Trusted Key

In order to have a very secure encrypted root filesystem we can use a trusted key to encrypt the disk; in fact, as we have seen in "The Trusted Key" section, we can ask the kernel to choose for us a random key with the following command:

```
$ keyctl add trusted fskey "new 32" @s | xargs keyctl pipe >
fskey.blob
$ cat fskey.blob
e794dae5e72cf9130ba19c746277e1f2836d3d2e103a0d7a47457fc6b790
322afe37bfc2
26c4466b20976cd7d9284f17d4ac439a9543a9565c51a68daa40746ef4ee4
0ae23f899d1
```

In this manner, we don't know the key value, and we have no way to get it even if we are the root user! Not only this, but this key is valid only when used by the CPU that created it.

This approach has undoubtedly advantages, but it also has the disadvantage that if the CPU that generated the key fails, all the disk contents are irretrievably lost; furthermore, it is not possible to generate an image of the root filesystem that is suitable for all the systems we want to produce (think, for example, in the case of mass production of a system—see the section "Producing a New System (Factory-Reset)" in Chapter 2).

Now, to make a real example, we can use again a loop device:

```
$ dd if=/dev/zero of=blockdev.bin bs=1M count=32
$ losetup /dev/loop0 blockdev.bin
```

Then, by using again the dmsetup command with proper key specification, we can create our encrypted block device:

```
$ dmsetup create cryptdev --table \
"0 $SECTORS crypt capi:cbc(aes)-plain :32:trusted:fskey 0 /dev/
loop0 0"
```

Note that this time we have used the /dev/loop0 device directly instead of asking the kernel to choose one for us, while the variable SECTORS has been set in the same manner as in the previous section via the blockdev command.

Note also that, in the case the above command hangs, as shown below when executed with the -vvv option argument to increase the verbosity:

```
$ dmsetup create -vvv cryptdev --table ...
...
...
dm create cryptdev  [ opencount flush ]   [16384] (*1)
dm cryptdev   (253:2) [ opencount flush ]   [16384] (*1)
dm resume cryptdev  [ opencount flush ]   [16384] (*1)
encdisk: Stacking NODE_ADD (253,2) 0:0 0600 [trust_udev]
```

```
Timestamp:         0.003179250 seconds
Udev cookie 0xd4da4ac (semid 1) decremented to 1
Udev cookie 0xd4da4ac (semid 1) waiting for zero
```

Here, the command will wait forever for zero, so we can use the
`--noudevsync` option argument to avoid any synchronization with
udev (that is what `dmsetup` does by default):

```
$ dmsetup create --noudevsync cryptdev --table ...
```

Now the command should execute correctly, but we must create by
ourselves the `cryptdev` node /dev/mapper by using the `mknodes`
subcommand, as reported below:

```
$ dmsetup mknodes cryptdev
```

This time the table entry has been changed in two important places:

1) `capi:cbc(aes)-plain`: The prefix `capi` is used to
   tell `dmsetup` to use the native syntax of the kernel's
   Crypto API to specify the algorithm and mode.

2) `:32:trusted:fskey`: Specifies that `dmsetup` must
   use the trusted key `fskey` which is 32 bytes long.
   Readers should note the colon (`:`) before the
   number 32; this is essential to indicate a kernel
   keyring key instead of a 64-character hex string for a
   raw key.

If everything works well, our `cryptdev` device should be available
under the /dev/mapper directory:

```
$ ls -l /dev/mapper/
total 0
crw------- 1 root root  10, 236 Aug 23 17:35 control
```

```
brw------- 1 root root 253,   1 Aug 23 17:39 cryptdev
brw------- 1 root root 253,   0 Aug 23 17:35 root
```

Now we can format the new block device as above and then mount it to be able to write files within it:

```
$ mkfs.ext4 /dev/mapper/cryptdev
mke2fs 1.47.0 (5-Feb-2023)
Creating filesystem with 32768 1k blocks and 8192 inodes
...
$ mount -t ext4 /dev/mapper/cryptdev /mnt/
[  290.498177] EXT4-fs (dm-1): mounted filesystem 8fa094eb-
dcd5-4edf-b34
0-f09d88b7cef0 r/w with ordered data mode. Quota mode: none.
$ echo "Very secret data" > /mnt/file.txt
$ umount /mnt/
[  333.982766] EXT4-fs (dm-1): unmounting filesystem 8fa094eb-
dcd5-4edf-b340-f09d88b7cef0.
```

All data are now correctly encrypted and saved. At this point, after a reboot, to mount our encrypted device again, we must load the trusted key as explained in the section "Using Trusted Key":

```
$ keyctl add trusted fskey "load $(cat fskey.blob)" @s
1021482817
$ losetup /dev/loop0 cryptdev.img
[  100.237944] loop0: detected capacity change from 0 to 65536
$ SECTORS=$(blockdev --getsz /dev/loop0)
$ dmsetup create cryptdev --table \
"0 $SECTORS crypt capi:cbc(aes)-plain :32:trusted:fskey 0 /dev/
loop0 0"
$ mount -t ext4 /dev/mapper/cryptdev /mnt/
[  146.135810] EXT4-fs (dm-1): mounted filesystem
09e2b78b-4db6-4eb2-897
```

```
6-04204fa3a2b7 r/w with ordered data mode. Quota mode: none.
$ cat /mnt/file.txt
Very secret data
```

This mechanism is really secure thanks to the kernel's help, which is the only one that knows the encryption key; however, this is also its main disadvantage in the case we need to create a ready-to-flash image of the entire system (think at the production stage, for example). To solve this issue (if we can call it an *issue*), we can use a logon key (see "The Logon Key" section), where we can specify the key payload, but be sure to define the key in a more secure environment than the root filesystem (e.g., within an initramfs as we will see in the section "A/B Schema" in Chapter 3).

Using Vendor-Specific Key

As already explained in the section "Vendor-Specific Keys," vendor-specific solutions can be fascinating and more secure than standard solutions. In this scenario, let's see how we can use CAAM-generated keys to create an encrypted block device.

The trick here is to use a logon key where we place the CAAM-generated key in such a way that the kernel will take the key and will pass it to the CAAM as is. Firstly, we have to generate the CAAM key as seen in the section "Vendor-Specific Keys":

```
$ caam-keygen create caamkey ecb -s 16
$ ls -l /etc/caam/
total 12
-rw-r--r-- 1 root root 36 Aug 23 15:57 caamkey
-rw-r--r-- 1 root root 96 Aug 23 15:57 caamkey.bb
```

Then we have to place the key to be passed to the CAAM within a logon key:

```
$ keyctl padd logon caamkey: @s < /etc/caam/caamkey
1043299630
```

And, of course, the `dmsetup` command must be altered to specify proper arguments to support this special key:

```
$ dmsetup create root --table \
"0 $SECTORS crypt capi:tk(cbc(aes))-plain :36:logon:caamkey: 0
/dev/loop0 0"
```

As above, the table entry has been changed in two important places:

1) `capi:tk(cbc(aes))-plain`: Since we are using a CAAM key we must specify the `tk(cbc(aes))` crypto algorithm to be sure the key is managed correctly.

2) `:36:logon:caamkey`: As underlined in "The Logon Key" section, the description for logon keys must be prefixed with a non-zero length string that describes the key subclass. So, please remember the last colon! Then this special key is 36 bytes long, and then this value must be reported as `:36`.

Note that if we need to know the encryption for some reason (e.g., to create a pre-built root filesystem image for production), we can create a well-known CAAM key with the `-t` option argument (as seen in the section "Vendor-Specific Keys"). For example:

```
$ caam-keygen create caamkey ecb -t
0123456789abcdef0123456789abcdef -h
```

This approach is really similar to the ones reported above, but with a higher security level given by the CAAM keys.

1.5 Summary

In this chapter, we have introduced the foundational elements of Linux cryptography, beginning with the **Linux Crypto API** and the **kernel keyring** for secure key management.

We have detailed the **AF_ALG socket interface**, which allows user-space applications to directly access the kernel's crypto layer, providing examples of its use with OpenSSL. The **crypto-afalg** tool was then introduced as a more secure solution that integrates the crypto API with Linux keyring management.

Finally, we have presented the **Linux Transparent Encryption** (used to encrypt data for user-space processes transparently).

Now that these concepts are clear, we can move to the next chapter to discover what Secure Boot is (and what it is NOT) in detail.

## CHAPTER 2

What Secure Boot Is (and What It Is NOT)

The **Secure Boot** is a set of rules and mechanisms designed to ensure that only trusted and authenticated software can run during the boot process of a computer. It acts as a *gatekeeper* that prevents unauthorized or malicious code from being loaded and executed before the *secure operating system* even starts. Secure Boot can also ensure that all (or at least the main significant) parts of the boot components are encrypted, so their contents are not readable either.

With the words *secure operating system*, we mean the code we want our system to run.

Before Secure Boot, systems typically used standard bootloaders, which offered little protection against malware that could infect or even replace the bootloader or kernel (or just the rootfs). Such malware could gain deep control over the system, making it very difficult to detect and remove.

Moreover, there were some circumstances where the software was extracted from a legitimate system and then executed on cloned hardware!

© Rodolfo Giometti 2026

R. Giometti, *Secure Boot Encryption with Linux*, Apress Pocket Guides,
https://doi.org/10.1007/979-8-8688-2818-8_2

The Secure Boot aims to solve this by creating a **Chain-of-Trust** from the moment the computer powers on by locking the software with the hardware in such a way that only legitimate software can be executed on legitimate hardware and vice versa.

Ultimately we can say that Secure Boot is

- *A mechanism that prevents unauthorized software from running on the system.* This is especially true regarding the bootloaders (companion software as the OP-TEE), the kernel, and, with some distinctions, the user-space programs.

- *A mechanism that prevents the cloning of a system by extracting legitimate software and running it on cloned hardware.*

- *A mechanism that prevents unauthorized access to the system's secrets when the system is in the power-off state.*

In this scenario, the Secure Boot is a powerful security feature, but it's also indispensable to understand what it isn't designed to do! In fact, it is strictly designed to protect the boot process by verifying the integrity of the software before the operating system fully loads. Its job is about verifying the integrity and authenticity of boot components until the mount of the encrypted rootfs. *Once the operating system is up and running, Secure Boot's job is done.*

So, once the system is up and running, it does not protect against malware that infects the system, such as viruses, ransomware, spyware, or phishing attacks. Moreover, it does not protect from DDoS, Man-in-the-Middle, or any other network attack. So, the usage of Secure Boot does not negate the need for using a firewall, being careful about what we download and run in the system, and backing up our data.

Moreover, we should consider that once the encrypted rootfs is mounted, from the process perspective it is a normal rootfs (with no encryption), so the rootfs encryption is an effective protection when the system is in the powered-off state!

The Secure Boot is a very specific guard, positioned right at the entrance of our computer's boot process. Its job is to make sure that only invited and verified guests (signed boot software) are allowed into the system, preventing unauthorized or malicious entities from getting in before anything else starts.

It's a foundational security layer, not a comprehensive security suite!

2.1 The Chain-of-Trust

We saw above that the Secure Boot is based on the concept of **Chain-of-Trust**, this special mechanism relies on cryptographic signatures and encryption. Each piece of boot software from the bootloaders (and their companion software), the kernel, and the rootfs must be digitally signed and encrypted with several private keys. The first component, the fundamental one, is the one that is trusted by default, and it is called **Root-of-Trust**. The Root of Trust cannot be verified by anything else in the system; its security is assumed because it is physically or logically protected. Usually, this is the ROM code fused into the chip.

Figure 2-1 tries to explain what we are going to describe.

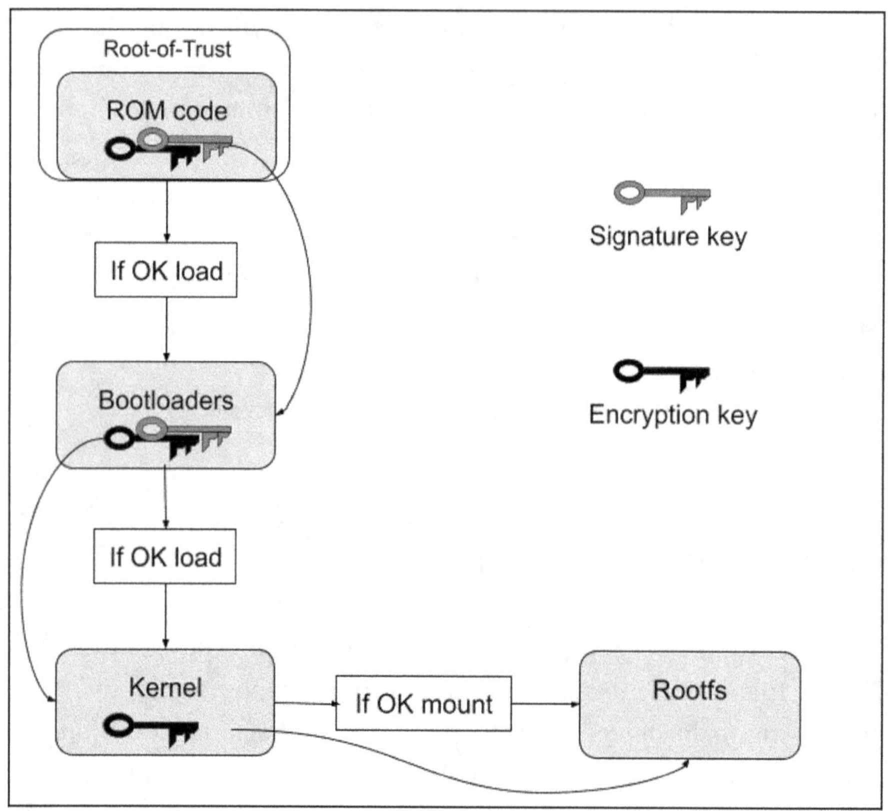

Figure 2-1. *The Chain-of-Trust*

When the system starts, the ROM code checks the digital signature of
the first piece of boot software it loads (that is a bootloader and, eventually,
one or more companion software specialized in cryptographic algorithms,
usually the OP-TEE—see below). If the signature of the initial boot software
is valid and matches a key in the chip (often this key is held within the
FUSEs—or non-volatile memory in general—in the chip), the ROM code
allows it to be decrypted and then executed. The bootloader then, in turn,
verifies the signature of the next component in the boot chain (the kernel,
in our case), eventually asking again for help from the companion software,
and if everything is OK, it decrypts the kernel and then executes it.

As the last step, the kernel, by using an encryption key, mounts the real rootfs. Readers should notice that in this last step the security is given by the encryption key only, since it's not possible to have a signed rootfs!

The reason we can't have a signed rootfs is derived from the fact the signature procedure is not as efficient as the encryption one. As seen in "The Block-Level Encryption" section in Chapter 1, an encrypted disk is implemented by doing a single block encryption, and this operation cannot be done for signing.

To solve this issue, developers may consider using other mechanisms that prevent the execution of all those program files that are properly signed, such as the Linux Integrity Measurement Architecture (IMA) at `https://sourceforge.net/p/linux-ima/wiki/Home/` which is not covered in this book.

For each stage, keys may change, and, in this case, the Chain-of-Trust is more robust; however, this mechanism is considered robust even in the case where we decide to use the same keys in each stage.

An improvement we can apply to the Chain-of-Trust is **tamper detection**. In other words, if a signature is invalid (or missing) or the hardware has been tampered with (e.g., by opening the enclosure where it's installed), Secure Boot will prevent the system from booting and often alert the user.

See Appendix A, "Notes on Tamper Detection," for further information about this mechanism.

2.2 The Boot Sequence

The Linux boot sequence is a complex but fascinating process, a carefully orchestrated dance of software and hardware that brings our operating system to life. While there can be variations depending on the used hardware and the specific bootloader or init system, the next figure reports a general overview of the typical stages, and the following sections report a brief description.

Firstly, we should keep in mind that Figure 2-2 is focused on ARM-based systems; in fact, with TF-A we mean the **ARM Trusted Firmware**, and the **OP-TEE** is a software component tightly coupled to the ARM architecture and the *TrustZone security extensions* (see below in this section for further information about these components). However, with minor changes, it can be assumed to be a general overview about a generic Linux boot sequence.

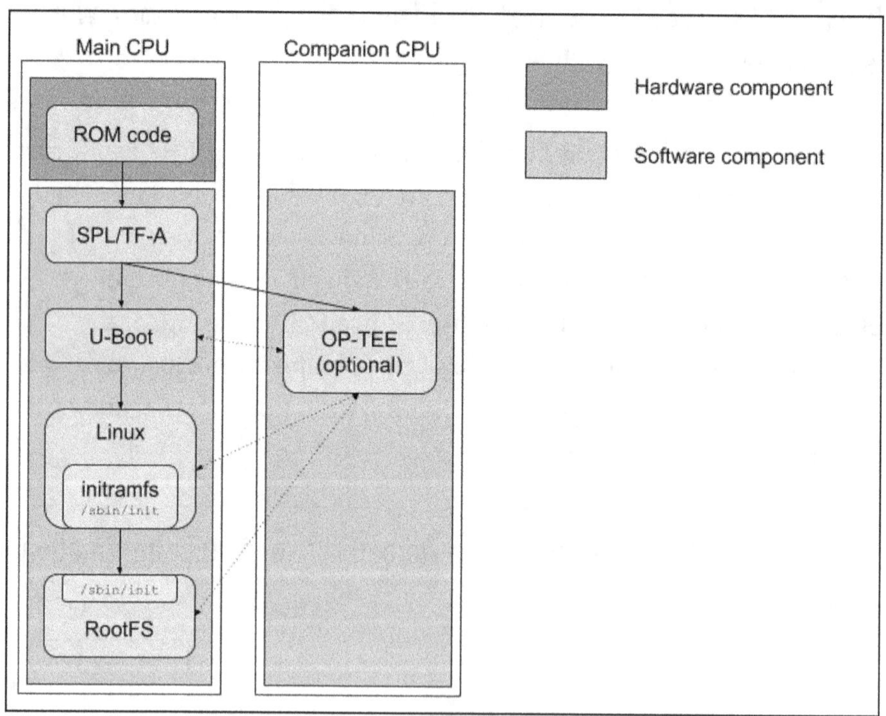

Figure 2-2. *The boot sequence for a generic Linux-based system*

At the power-on, the ROM boot code starts, and, after performing some initialization, it loads the bootloader (or the prebootloader according to the specific system characteristics) from a mass storage device and then executes it.

Since the ROM code is the set of instructions, programs, or data that is pre-programmed or burned into a ROM chip, it cannot be changed, and then it is the only component that is considered *secure* (at least from the Secure Boot perspective).

The situation changes when we consider the other components that must be secured to get a secure system.

2.2.1 Booting

Modern systems use dynamic RAM (DRAM), which is not ready to be used at power-on. It's an uninitialized raw state, and the CPU cannot simply load programs into it or execute code from it until the DRAM controller is configured and the DRAM chips themselves are properly set up (timings, refresh rates, voltage levels, etc.). That's why we need something like a **prebootloader** to initialize DRAM (and other essential hardware) so that larger, more complex code (in our example, the real bootloader, but in some systems even the kernel!) can be loaded and executed from it.

On the other hand, if our system has an already usable DRAM, the ROM boot can load and execute the bootloader, which (after doing other important settings for the boot) is charged to load the kernel from a mass storage device and then executes it.

In our case, the bootloader is U-Boot and the prebootloader is the **Secondary Program Loader (SPL)**, but this may vary... in fact, modern systems use other components that are executed in this step. We refer to the **ARM Trusted Firmware** (usually named as **ATF** or, more frequently, **TF-A**) and the **Open Portable Trusted Execution Environment (OP-TEE)**.

The OP-TEE (for ARM Cortex-A) is primarily designed to run as a companion to a non-secure Linux kernel utilizing ARM TrustZone technology. OP-TEE's main purpose is to enable secure processing for critical applications and data on devices. It allows developers to build *Trusted Applications* (TAs) that run exclusively within the Secure World, protecting them from malware or vulnerabilities in the Normal World OS.

To briefly explain better, we can say that a Trusted Execution Environment (TEE) is a secure, isolated environment that runs alongside a Rich Execution Environment (REE), which is typically a normal operating system like a Linux-based distro such as Ubuntu or Debian (or Android, Windows, etc.). The ARM TrustZone hardware technology divides a single physical processor into two isolated *worlds*:

- *Secure World*: This is where TEE OP-TEE runs. It's highly protected by hardware mechanisms, ensuring that code and data within it are confidential and their integrity is maintained, even if the normal world is compromised.

- *Normal World*: This is where Linux runs. It has full access to most of the system's resources but cannot directly access or tamper with the Secure World's resources.

This isolation is achieved through hardware-enforced memory separation, protected registers, and controlled entry/exit points (via the Secure Monitor, often implemented by ARM Trusted Firmware). It's very common that OP-TEE runs on a different CPU inside the same chip (see `https://optee.readthedocs.io/en/latest/` for further detailed information).

The terms ARM Trusted Firmware (ATF) and Trusted Firmware-A (TF-A) are indeed interchangeable, and they refer to a critical piece of firmware for ARMv8-A and ARMv9-A architectures. Its primary role is to establish and maintain a Trusted Execution Environment (TEE) by running at the highest privilege level, acting as a **secure monitor** (see `https://trustedfirmware-a.readthedocs.io/en/latest/` for further detailed information).

From our perspective, we can say that the main target of TF-A is to load U-Boot and (optionally) the OP-TEE and execute them. While OP-TEE lives in its secured world, U-Boot, in the normal world, does its settings and then loads and executes the kernel, eventually asking for cryptographic help from OP-TEE.

For example, on an iMX8 machine we can get the following messages:

```
U-Boot SPL 2024.04-imx_v2024.04_6.6.36-2.1.0+g476cc38e7e+p0
(Aug 07 2025 - 07:48:44 +0000)
DDRINFO: start DRAM init
DDRINFO: DRAM rate 4000MTS
DDRINFO:ddrphy calibration done
DDRINFO: ddrmix config done
SECO:  RNG instantiated
Normal Boot
Trying to boot from BOOTROM
Boot Stage: Primary boot
image offset 0x8000, pagesize 0x200, ivt offset 0x0

Authenticate image from DDR location 0x401fadc0...
NOTICE:  Do not release JR0 to NS as it can be used by HAB
NOTICE:  BL31: v2.10.0  (release):automotive-15.0.0_1.1.0
NOTICE:  BL31: Built : 08:52:12, Nov  4 2024
...
```

This section is related to the SPL prebootloader. Readers should notice the following message:

```
Authenticate image from DDR location 0x401fadc0...
```

Once the ROM code has checked the SPL, then in turn it checks the U-Boot and OP-TEE images (the next images to be loaded) before continuing. Then, all lines prefixed with NOTICE come from OP-TEE and then the boot continues with the following messages from the real bootloader:

```
...
U-Boot 2024.04-imx_v2024.04_6.6.36-2.1.0+g476cc38e7e+p0 (Aug 07
2025 - 0 7:48:44 +0000)

CPU:   i.MX8MP[8] rev1.1 1600 MHz (running at 1200 MHz)
CPU:   Industrial temperature grade (-40C to 105C) at 48C
Reset cause: POR
Model: board i.MX8MPlus iCore Plus
DRAM:  4 GiB
optee optee: OP-TEE api uid mismatch
Core:  76 devices, 27 uclasses, devicetree: separate
MMC:   FSL_SDHC: 1, FSL_SDHC: 2
Loading Environment from MMC... OK
In:    serial
Out:   serial
Err:   serial
SECO:  RNG instantiated
switch to partitions #0, OK
mmc2(part 0) is current device
SOF:   0
flash target is MMC:2
Net:   eth1: ethernet@30bf0000 [PRIME]
Fastboot: Normal
Normal Boot
Hit any key to stop autoboot:  0
starting USB...
```

```
Bus usb@38100000: Register 2000140 NbrPorts 2
Starting the controller
USB XHCI 1.10
Bus usb@38200000: Register 2000140 NbrPorts 2
Starting the controller
USB XHCI 1.10
scanning bus usb@38100000 for devices... 1 USB Device(s) found
scanning bus usb@38200000 for devices... 2 USB Device(s) found
        scanning usb for storage devices... 0 Storage
        Device(s) found

Device 0: unknown device
MMC: no card present
switch to partitions #0, OK
mmc2(part 0) is current device
...
75301040 bytes read in 238 ms (301.7 MiB/s)
Booting from mmc ...

...
```

These messages are produced by U-Boot and we can see it tries to enable some interfaces, trying to locate a kernel image to start.

It's interesting to note that in this example, the bootloader is just signed and not encrypted. This is not a problem for the Secure Boot since it doesn't break the Chain-of-Trust (a signature is present), and this bootloader doesn't hold any sensible information, so even if the code is in plain text, it is only the bootloader code and not the application program.

On the other hand, if the bootloader holds some sensible information (e.g., an encryption key or a password), it must be protected by encrypting the whole bootloader or, at least, by hashing or wrapping this crucial information. Or the Chain-of-Trust will be broken!

When a valid fitimage (that the file holding the kernel image, the Device-Tree and other useful information for booting) is found, the bootloader prints `Booting from mmc ...` and then:

```
...
Authenticate image from DDR location 0x40400000...

Secure boot enabled

HAB Configuration: 0xcc, HAB State: 0x99
No HAB Events Found!
...
```

This is another authentication step. In fact, before executing the kernel fitimage, U-Boot checks its signature and then decrypts it. If everything goes well, we get the usual booting message, as shown below:

```
...
## Loading kernel from FIT Image at 40400000 ...
   Using 'conf-0' configuration
   Verifying Hash Integrity ... OK
   Trying 'kernel' kernel subimage
     Description:  Linux kernel [Image-initramfs-imx8mp-
                   icore.bin]
     Created:      2025-08-22  16:30:12 UTC
     Type:         Kernel Image
     Compression:  uncompressed
     Data Start:   0x40400124
     Data Size:    75158016 Bytes = 71.7 MiB
```

```
     Architecture: AArch64
     OS:           Linux
     Load Address: 0x50000000
     Entry Point:  0x50000000
     Hash algo:    crc32
     Hash value:   87b1934a
   Verifying Hash Integrity ... crc32+ OK
## Loading fdt from FIT Image at 40400000 ...
   Using 'conf-0' configuration
   Verifying Hash Integrity ... OK
   Trying 'fdt-0' fdt subimage
     Description:  Flattened Device Tree [imx8mp-icore.dtb]
     Created:      2025-08-22  16:30:12 UTC
     Type:         Flat Device Tree
     Compression:  uncompressed
     Data Start:   0x44bad420
     Data Size:    62818 Bytes = 61.3 KiB
     Architecture: AArch64
     Load Address: 0x45000000
     Hash algo:    crc32
     Hash value:   e66a2c9e
   Verifying Hash Integrity ... crc32+ OK
   Loading fdt from 0x44bad420 to 0x45000000
   Booting using the fdt blob at 0x45000000
Working FDT set to 45000000
   Loading Kernel Image to 50000000
   Using Device Tree in place at 0000000045000000, end
0000000045012561
Working FDT set to 45000000

Starting kernel ...
```

A valid fitimage is now executed, and after the message `Starting kernel ...` the CPU is executing the Linux code.

2.2.2 Starting the Kernel

Once the kernel starts, it sets up all the system's components and devices, and then it does the two last steps: mounting the root filesystem (rootfs) and then executing the `init` process (which, on modern systems, typically is **Systemd**).

In our case, the kernel is Linux, and the booting messages continue as reported below:

```
...
[    0.000000] Booting Linux on physical CPU 0x0000000000
[0x410fd034]
[    0.000000] Linux version 6.6.52-gebea7e7c2b53 (oe-user@oe-
host) (aarch64-poky-linux-gcc (GCC) 13.3.0, GNU ld (GNU
Binutils) 2.42.0.20240723)
 #1 SMP PREEMPT Fri Aug 22 15:04:30 UTC 2025
[    0.000000] KASLR disabled due to lack of seed
[    0.000000] Machine model: board i.Core i.MX8M Plus
...
[    0.000000] Kernel command line: console=ttymxc1,115200
device=/dev/mmcblk2 root=/dev/mmcblk2p4 rootwait rw initramfs_
normal boot_schema=a_b root_name=root_b
[    0.000000] Unknown kernel command line parameters
"initramfs_normal device=/dev/mmcblk2 boot_schema=a_b root_
name=root_b", will be passed to user space.
...
```

Usually, the bootloader exchanges some information with the kernel by using the so-called **kernel command line**. Readers should consider something as the bootloader executes the kernel by executing it from a hypothetical command line. Looking at the above output, it is as if someone has written the command below on the bootloader command line:

```
uboot> fitimage console=ttymxc1,115200 device=/dev/mmcblk2
root=/dev/mmcblk2p4 rootwait rw initramfs_normal boot_
schema=a_b root_name=root_b
```

In this manner, the kernel parses the command line and gathers information about how to continue the boot.

What the above settings mean will be explained in detail later in this book. Also, readers may consult the section "Fixing the Kernel Command Line" in Appendix B to see how to protect this information.

2.2.3 Entering the Root Filesystem

The root filesystem, abbreviated as *rootfs*, is the highest-level directory in the Linux (and Unix-like) filesystem hierarchy. It is denoted by a single forward slash (/) and it is the central hub of your entire Linux operating system. Every other file and directory on our system, whether it's on the same physical disk or a different one, is logically mounted (or connected) under the root filesystem.

The rootfs is normally located on a mass storage, and the kernel can mount it directly, but modern OSs (based on Linux) prefer doing an intermediate step before effectively mounting this *final* rootfs; that is, they use an initial RAM filesystem (typically referred to as **initramfs**).

An initramfs is a small, temporary, in-memory root filesystem that the Linux kernel uses during its early boot stages, before the real root filesystem (the one containing our entire operating system) can be mounted. Think of it as a small, self-contained mini-operating system whose sole purpose is to help the main operating system get started. It can be located on a mass storage, but it's quite usual that it is encapsulated within the kernel itself.

The initramfs is useful when special tasks must be accomplished before mounting the real rootfs; for example, if the rootfs is stored on a RAID system or in the case where we have to update the whole rootfs before executing it; simply speaking, in all such circumstances where the real rootfs is not directly accessible by the kernel.

Once the initramfs has done all the needed steps to retrieve the real rootfs, the init process in the initramfs does the `switch_root` command to do the transition to the *real* root filesystem that contains the real (or complete) operating system and the real `init` process.

To briefly explain this concept, we can say that once the real rootfs has been retrieved and then mounted into the `real_rootfs` directory, we can *jump* into it and execute its `/sbin/init` process by doing the following commands:

```
exec switch_root /real_rootfs /sbin/init
```

This command effectively does the switch between the current root (within the initramfs) and the real root (within the real, or complete, root filesystem). We can get further information by reading its manpages (man 8 switch_root):

```
SWITCH_ROOT(8)                 System Administration
          SWITCH_ROOT(8)

NAME
       switch_root - switch to another filesystem as the root
       of the mount tree

SYNOPSIS
       switch_root [-hV]

       switch_root newroot init [arg...]
```

DESCRIPTION

> switch_root moves already mounted /proc, /dev, /sys
> and /run to newroot and makes newroot the new root
> filesystem and starts init process.

> WARNING: switch_root removes recursively all files and
> directories on the current root filesystem.

...

The reader should carefully note the fact that (as reported above) switch_root removes recursively all files and directories on the current root filesystem. This is an important step in order to get the old root isolation; that is, the initramfs (the old root) will become inaccessible to the newly booting system, and it can optionally be unmounted and will simply disappear when that memory is reclaimed. This fact is critical because the initramfs occupied RAM, and its contents are no longer needed, but also it can hold information that we don't want to share with the real rootfs!

Before ending this section, we should underline two important concepts:

1) Readers should not confuse the switch_root command with the chroot command; they are entirely different commands! The former is a system-wide operation that profoundly alters the system's fundamental environment specifically designed for the boot process to transition from a temporary root to the permanent one. It also changes the root filesystem for the *entire running kernel* and handles the relocation/isolation of the old root filesystem.

While `chroot` just changes the root directory *for a specific process and its children, it is* typically used for isolated environments (e.g., building software, repairing a broken system, network daemons, etc.) without affecting other running processes. By using it, the kernel's actual root filesystem for the entire system remains unchanged, and it does not involve moving the old root or cleaning it up.

2)   The command `switch_root` is executed by the shell with the `exec` keyword. It's an essential step! In fact, the `exec  <cmd>` in a Unix-like shell (like Bash) replaces the current shell process with the command specified, without creating a new process. When we run `<cmd>`, the shell forks a new process and then waits for the command to complete, while when we run `exec  <cmd>`, the shell itself transforms into `<cmd>`! The shell process (and its PID) is replaced by the image of the command `<cmd>`. No new process is created, and the shell never resumes!

In this situation it's quite obvious why this behavior is really critical; in fact, we must be sure that the init process within the real root filesystem has the PID 1 (as a well-functioning `init` process would have).

Below is reported an example of what the kernel prints during this step:

```
...
[    3.521508] Freeing unused kernel memory: 43456K
[    3.526221] Run /init as init process
...
```

```
[    3.644601] EXT4-fs (mmcblk2p1): mounted filesystem
f2bfad6c-b3c9-4037-962a-a9065f7cc929 r/w with ordered data
mode. Quota mode: none.
[    3.670644] EXT4-fs (mmcblk2p1): unmounting filesystem
f2bfad6c-b3c9-4037-962a-a9065f7cc929.
937875274
222247019
init: checking rootfs on /dev/mapper/root...
e2fsck 1.47.0 (5-Feb-2023)
root: clean, 17913/256000 files, 228590/1024000 blocks
init: mounting rootfs on /dev/mapper/root...
[    3.801532] EXT4-fs (dm-0): mounted filesystem
e021413f-2f93-4471-844
3-e0f5704b1f07 r/w with ordered data mode. Quota mode: none.
init: entering rootfs on /dev/mapper/root...
...
```

As we can see, the kernel starts init which in turn mounts the rootfs
on /dev/mapper/root. This is not a usual block device (such as /dev/
sda1, /dev/mmcblk2, or /dev/mtd5), but it is a special block device that
implements the root filesystem encryption.

How it can be implemented will be explained in detail in Chapter 3.

Subsequently, the boot continues as usual, and the init in the initramfs
is replaced by the real init process, which is systemd in our example:

```
...
[    4.319682] systemd[1]: systemd 255.18^ running in system
mode (+PAM-AUDIT -SELINUX -APPARMOR +IMA -SMACK +SECCOMP
-GCRYPT -GNUTLS -OPENSSL+ACL +BLKID -CURL -ELFUTILS -FIDO2
 IDN2  IDN -IPTC +KMOD -LIBCRYPTSETUP +LIBFDISK -PCRE2
```

```
-PWQUALITY -P11KIT -QRENCODE -TPM2 -BZIP2 -LZ4 -XZ -ZL IB
+ZSTD -BPF_FRAMEWORK +XKBCOMMON +UTMP +SYSVINIT default-
hierarchy=uni fied)
[    4.351695] systemd[1]: Detected architecture arm64.

Welcome to BNDL Distro with XWayland 6.6-scarthgap (scarthgap)!
...
```

Then Systemd starts all needed components, and the boot ends:

```
...
[  OK  ] Started Session c1 of User root.
[   11.643582] weston[392]: memfd_create() called without
MFD_EXEC or MFD_NOEXEC_SEAL set [  OK  ] Started Weston, a
Wayland compositor, as a system service.
[   13.536964] i2c 1-004c: deferred probe pending

BNDL Distro with XWayland 6.6-scarthgap imx8mp-icore-
devel ttymxc1

imx8mp-icore-devel login:
...
```

Note that, for simplicity, we have reported above the console prompt, but, of course, the system can start with a graphical interface (the Weston).

Before closing this section, we underline again that the Chain-of-Trust assures that in each stage the correct software is executed, but regarding the root filesystem this is true for the filesystem as a whole and not for each program in it! In fact, the Chain-of-Trust may stop if the rootfs is not correctly encrypted, but once the mount is executed, from the process perspective, the filesystem is in plain text, and then nobody checks for the validity of each program, starting from the /sbin/init process.

2.3 Producing a New System (Factory-Reset)

Until now we have considered a system running in its normal state: the main programs are active, all configurations are effective, and everything works as it used to.

However, every system has a factory production stage; that is, that critical process that involves dedicated equipment and follows a specific sequence to ensure the correct software is loaded and the board is functional. Typically, this step is also called **firmware programming** or flashing.

When a board has been assembled with all its components, it is a blank slate, and a firmware (the software that controls the hardware) must be loaded in the board's non-volatile memory (for Linux-based systems, this kind of memory is often flash memory).

Programming a blank slate system is not a hard task, but when the Secure Boot is involved, we must take care of some aspects!

Firstly, we should consider that all the firmware images must be properly signed and (hopefully) encrypted. Only nonsensible data can be in a plain text form or not signed. Then we must also program the CPU to enter into its secure state, and then the proper signature key and (hopefully) encryption key must be fused too within the CPU itself.

All these best practices are commonly named **Software Secure Provisioning** (SSP).

2.3.1 Production in an In-House Environment

If the factory production stage is done in-house, we can use a simplified production procedure, and a typical one may be composed of the following steps:

1) The CPU does a normal boot and loads (via serial or USB interface) an initial code. Typically, a special U-Boot release is properly configured to execute all needed commands in this stage.

2) The initial code programs the needed keys into the FUSEs and checks that everything is OK.

3) If so, the code programs the flash memory with the initial firmware release and then does a reboot.

4) The CPU now executes into a secure state and loads the secure bootloader, and the boot with the Chain-of-Trust begins.

The above steps may change a bit according to the specific CPU used; however, what is reported here is very common.

About step 1, we can note that we may use an unsigned bootloader due to the fact we are the ones who actually do the step, and we can assume that no malicious software is used. However, step 2 is a bit more delicate; in fact, during this step some critical keys are involved.

For example, consider the bootloaders and kernel encryption key. Even if we are in a (relatively) secure environment, the possibility that the encryption key is exposed on the communication channel is at risk (e.g., serial buses can be easily read by cheap instrumentation). In this situation, we can imagine implementing a specific cryptographic **Key-Agreement**

Protocol within the bootloader so it can exchange data in a secure form with a remote server that manages the factory production.

A possible protocol can be the Diffie–Hellman exchange protocol, which allows two parties, who have no prior knowledge of each other, to establish a shared secret key over an otherwise insecure communication channel (see Figure 2-3).

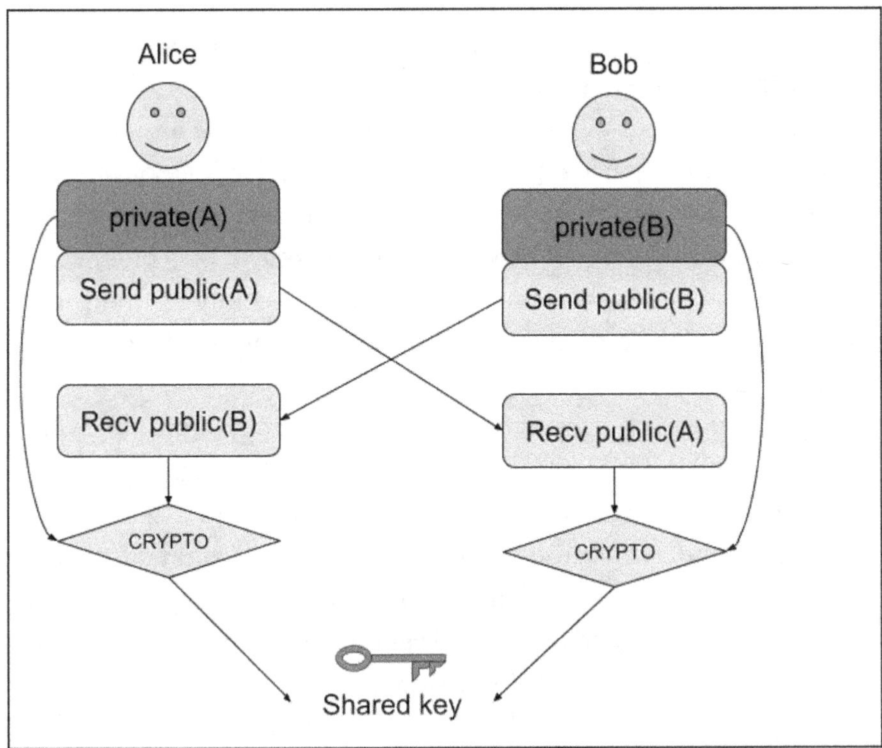

Figure 2-3. How the Diffie–Hellman exchange protocol works

Once the sensible data has been transferred and properly fused in the new system (step 3), we can safely restart in secure mode (step 4), and everything can proceed without problems.

This procedure can be easily implemented on almost all CPUs, while the critical point is that no malicious software or hardware is used to steal secrets during the FUSEs programming.

2.3.2 Production in a Third-Party Environment

On the other hand, if we decide to produce our system in a third-party factory, the suppositions done in the previous section (especially the one about the first step) fall. In fact, even if we use a KPP protocol to protect key exchange, we have no guarantees about which initial code is executed at the above step 1! Moreover, even if we can have some assurance that the initial code is not evil, we have no guarantees that such software is actually executed on malicious hardware!

Consider this scenario: we've decided to outsource the production of our boards to a third-party supplier, and to ensure the initial software is what we want, we've provided this company with special hardware capable of delivering our code at boot time for every new system they produce. Once this is done, using this same system, we begin communicating with the new device to be programmed and then send it the keys it needs to write to the fuses.

Well, but who can assure us that we're actually communicating with a new device and not with malicious hardware that, by mimicking the communication protocol, is simply trying to steal our keys?

The only option is to use an authentication system within the ROM code! In fact, the ROM code is considered secure by default, and by using a special certificate provided by the CPU vendor, we can be sure that we are effectively speaking with a genuine system.

Actually, this is not strictly true. In fact, we can have some situations where we can solve the problem by doing a pre-phase where we use a signed bootloader to write FUSES. But this is not a general solution out of the scope of this book.

In this scenario, a typical production stage may be composed of the following steps:

1) The target CPU does a protected boot, and the ROM code sends its certificate holding public key.

2) Once the host has verified the certificate with a specific Certificate Authority (usually a public key from the CPU vendor), it answers to the target with its public key.

3) Now the secure channel can be created by using the generated shared key, and the host can safely send the needed keys to the target ROM code, which in turn proceeds with the FUSEs programming.

4) Once finished, the target CPU can reboot in a secure state, and the factory production can go ahead without any concerns.

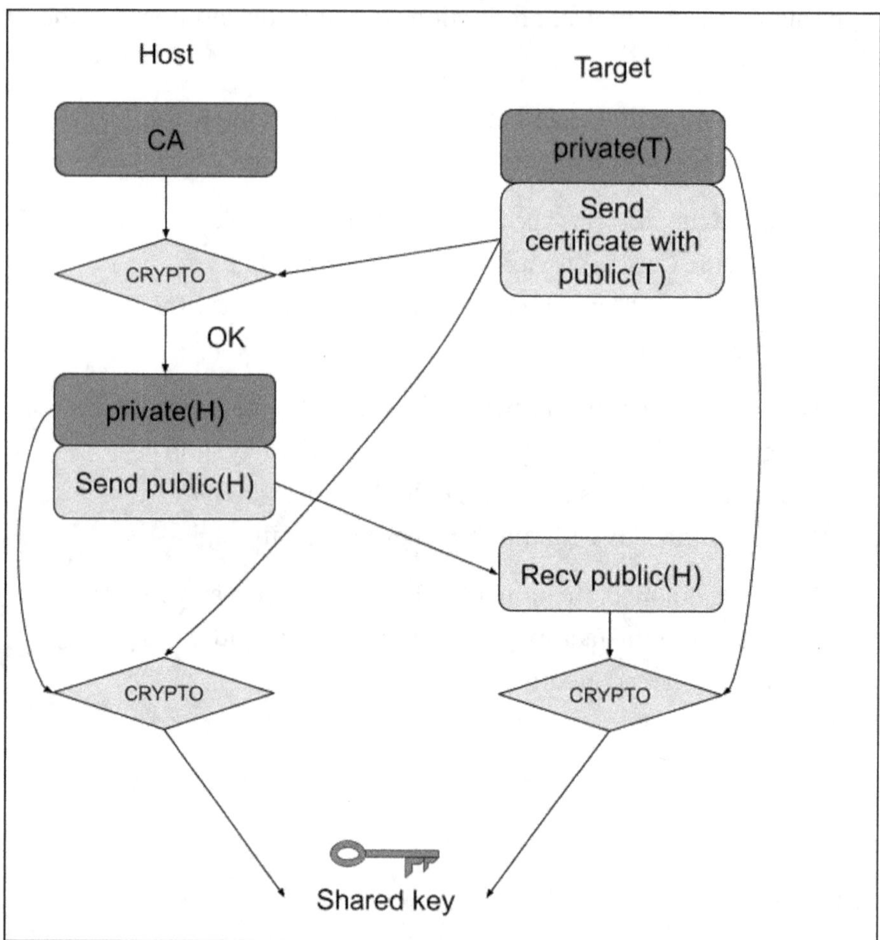

Figure 2-4. *The key-agreement protocol primitive in the ROM code*

Note that the procedure in Figure 2-4 is very similar to the one in the previous section, but it requires specific support by the CPU, and not all CPUs can do it.

2.3.3 The Initial Root Filesystem

When we discussed the Chain-of-Trust, we stated that all images must be properly signed and (hopefully) encrypted. We can also imagine producing a binary flash image where everything is in place that can be simply programmed within the mass storage of our system; however, a problem may arise when we have to create the encrypted rootfs.

We have seen in "The Block-Level Encryption" section in Chapter 1 that usually the rootfs is encrypted with a random key, which usually is not known to the developers either! So, it's obvious that we cannot prebuild a valid image for it. Furthermore, even if we perfectly know the encryption key, there is still the difficulty that on some CPUs this key is often sealed, and this operation produces different binaries for each CPU (since the sealing operation depends on a unique master key for each CPU).

To address this issue, the best thing to do is to provide an initial root filesystem as a simple archive (typically a compressed TAR), and during the first boot, the system automatically creates the encrypted rootfs and copies all files into it. In this scenario, the encryption key of this initial rootfs can be stored in a secure form within the kernel image (e.g., in the initramfs of an encrypted fitimage—see Figure 2-5).

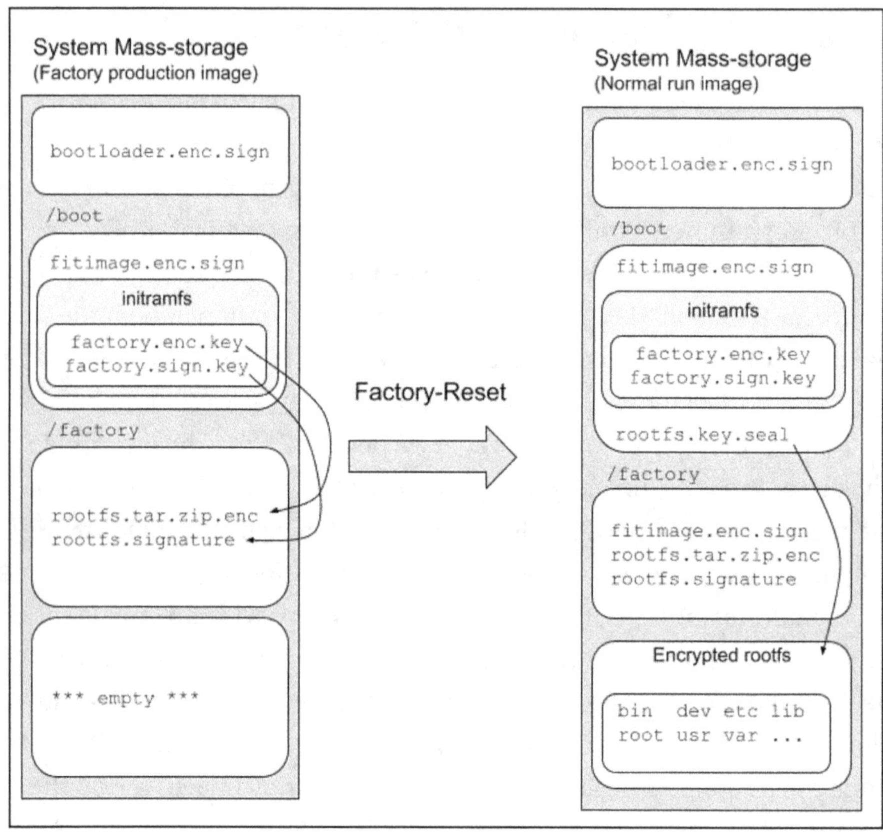

Figure 2-5. *The factory-reset evolution*

As we can see in the above figure, usually within the factory production flash image, we have

- A bootloader(s) image that is signed and (hopefully) encrypted. This image usually is not held in a partition, but it's written at some specific offsets within the mass storage disk.

- A fitimage image that is both signed and encrypted. This image holds the kernel, which in turn embeds the initramfs where the encryption (`factory.enc.key`) and public signature (`rootfs.sign.key`) keys for the factory rootfs are located.

- A rootfs image as a TAR archive, both signed and encrypted, which holds the rootfs files to be installed into the future encrypted rootfs partition. In the figure, this compressed and signed image archive has been named `rootfs.tar.zip.enc`, while with the `rootfs.signature` we have addressed the relative digital signature; however, we can use a single file where the signature is appended (in this case we can name the file as `rootfs.tar.zip.enc.sign`).

The bootloader loads, checks, and then executes the fitimage. The kernel within the fitimage starts and executes the `init` process in the embedded initramfs, which checks the rootfs signature and, if successful, decrypts and installs the rootfs files into a newly created crypted rootfs partition.

Now it should be clear why it is critical that the fitimage must be encrypted; this is because the encryption key needed to decrypt the TAR archive is usually placed into the initramfs.

The key used to generate the encrypted rootfs is stored, in a sealed form, in the `/factory` partition (or any other plain text partition) to be used at every system boot. Note that generating and then sealing this key is not an issue since all operations are done by the CPU that actually uses them and not on a generic host.

2.4 Updating the System (System-Update)

Every embedded application should consider a proper way to update itself. And doing an update in a system with the Secure Boot introduces the implication that we must consider some precautions (even if less restrictive than ones in the factory-reset).

Firstly, all firmware images must be properly signed and encrypted with the right keys, or the update may fail or, worse, the system will hang! A typical update can be an archive composed of the bootloader image (`bootloader.enc.sign`, if needed), the fitimage image (`fitimage.enc.sign`), and the rootfs as a compressed TAR archive (again as two separate files: `rootfs.tar.zip.enc` the compressed and signed image archive, and `rootfs.signature` the rootfs digital signature). Figure 2-6 shows this configuration.

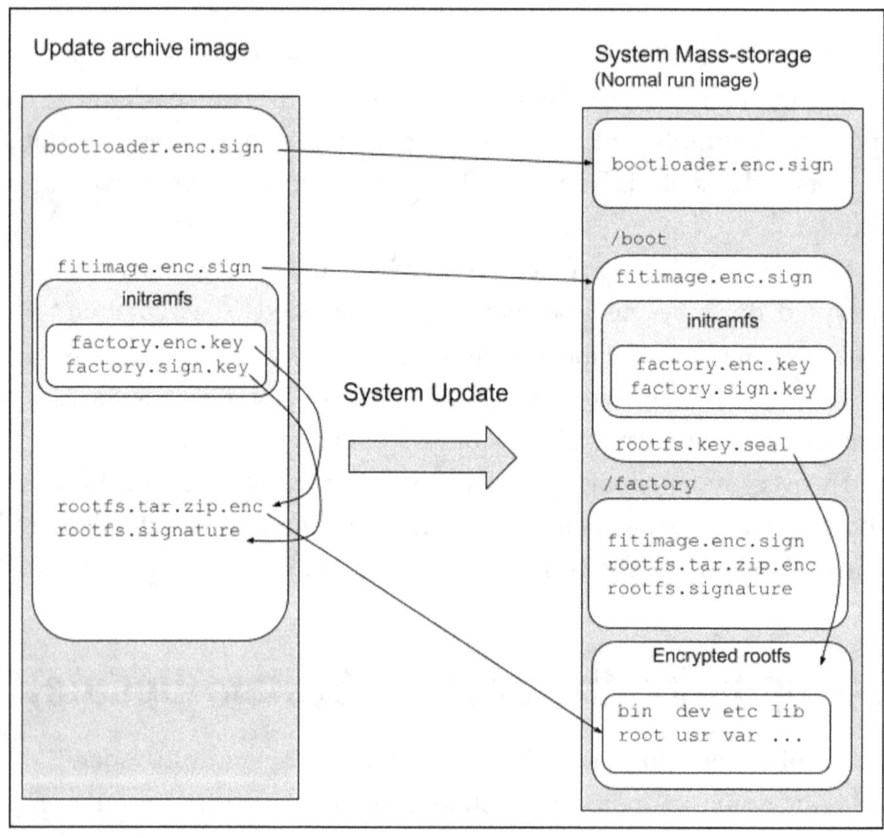

Figure 2-6. *The system-update evolution*

To update the rootfs, we must get access to the encryption key used to encrypt the rootfs TAR archive and (in some circumstances) also the encryption key used to encrypt the running rootfs where these files must be installed. Getting access to the latter key, that is, the key used to encrypt the running rootfs, is not an issue since it is in a sealed form within the /boot directory; a little more delicate is the issue about how to access the rootfs TAR archive encryption key in a way that the key is not exposed in the filesystem.

This difficulty is related to the way we decide to implement the system, and everything will be clearer later in this book when we are going to present the different booting schemas we can have in our system.

For the moment the reader should keep in mind that this key must be managed properly to prevent unwanted access.

2.5 Summary

In this chapter, we have seen what **Secure Boot** is by introducing the concept of **Chain-of-Trust** and explaining the boot sequence in detail.

We detailed the Linux boot sequence, focusing on ARM-based systems and the roles of components like the SPL, U-Boot, **ARM Trusted Firmware (TF-A)** acting as a secure monitor, and the **Open Portable Trusted Execution Environment (OP-TEE)** for Secure World isolation. We have also introduced what we should keep in mind when we wish to produce a secured system (in-house or in a third-party factory) or when we distribute a system update in order to prevent possible corruption of the Chain-of-Trust or the system's secrets exploitation. Now we are ready to move to the next chapter, where we are going to present how a real implementation works to better understand how we can implement all Secure Boot concepts within our systems.

CHAPTER 3

Real Implementations

Linux-based OSs can be installed within extremely diverse systems, starting from a normal desktop (or laptop) PC, passing to smartphones, WiFi access points, smart TVs, or into very unexpected locations like trains, electrical cabinets, or medical devices. In these last devices, we must be sure that the system can be recovered and updated reliably without any user intervention (or at least with very little specialized support). To achieve this, all the system components must be carefully placed in the system's mass storage device (or devices) in order to guarantee a reliable and secure recovery or update.

In the previous section, we presented all the boot components, and here we can show how we can organize them within the system. At the time of the writing of this book, the most used mass storage device is eMMC, even if we can still find NOR or NAND equipped devices or a mix of them (NOR + eMMC or NAND + eMMC).

The term eMMC stands for **embedded MultiMediaCard**. Essentially, it is a type of NAND flash memory used for storage in portable devices and embedded systems. The difference between raw NAND flash is that it also integrates a controller and an interface into a single package, making it a compact and efficient storage solution that, from the point-of-view of the final user, it is just like a hard disk.

© Rodolfo Giometti 2026

R. Giometti, *Secure Boot Encryption with Linux*, Apress Pocket Guides,
https://doi.org/10.1007/979-8-8688-2818-8_3

Linux assigns a device name to the eMMC which typically follows the pattern /dev/mmcblkX, where X is a number that identifies the specific device. For example, below is reported the boot messages from a real device equipped with an eMMC:

```
[     1.951701] mmc2: SDHCI controller on 30b60000.mmc
    [30b60000.mmc] using ADMA
[     2.045162] mmc2: new HS400 Enhanced strobe MMC card at
    address 0001
[     2.056698] mmcblk2: mmc2:0001 AJTD4R 14.6 GiB
[     2.072162]  mmcblk2: p1 p2 p3 p4 p5 p6
[     2.087359] mmcblk2boot0: mmc2:0001 AJTD4R 4.00 MiB
[     2.094348] mmcblk2boot1: mmc2:0001 AJTD4R 4.00 MiB
[     2.109907] mmcblk2rpmb: mmc2:0001 AJTD4R 4.00 MiB,
    chardev (235:0)
```

In the above messages we can notice that, like other storage devices, an eMMC can be divided into partitions (p1, p2, etc.), all represented as separate block devices with names like /dev/mmcblk2p1, /dev/mmcblk2p2 and so on.

Note the p followed by a number indicates the partition number, which is quite different from the partition identifications for hard disks, such as /dev/sdb1, /dev/sdb2, etc.

However, apart from these common aspects, we should also notice the devices named mmcblk2boot0 and mmcblk2boot1, these devices are eMMC's special boot areas. These are typically used for storing the bootloader and other firmware needed to start the system and are special because they are guaranteed to be more reliable than ordinary areas.

As a last note, the device mmcblk2rpmb is the *Replay-Protected Memory Block (RPMB)*, which is another secure area for storing sensitive data, such as encryption keys, securely via encryption.

The RPMB secure area is not covered in this book, and curious readers may get further information about how to use it, for example, with OP-TEE at https://optee.readthedocs.io/en/3.16.0/ architecture/secure_storage.html.

Once the system is up and running, the eMMC acts as a normal hard disk, and we can get some information about its partitioning by using the lsblk command as shown below:

```
# lsblk /dev/mmcblk2
NAME            MAJ:MIN  RM  SIZE   RO TYPE MOUNTPOINTS
mmcblk2         179:0    0   14.6G  0  disk
|-mmcblk2p1     179:1    0   256M   0  part /boot
|-mmcblk2p2     179:2    0     8M   0  part /factory
|-mmcblk2p3     179:3    0   3.9G   0  part
|-mmcblk2p4     179:4    0   3.9G   0  part
| `-root        253:0    0   3.9G   0  dm   /
|-mmcblk2p5     179:5    0   1000M  0  part /data
`-mmcblk2p6     179:6    0   3.9G   0  part
```

An attentive reader will surely have noticed that the rootfs, which is marked with the slash (/) character, is not mounted on a raw partition, but it is mounted on the special root partition instead, which is connected to mmcblk2p4. We are going to explain this better further in this book; for the moment, the important thing to know is that such configuration is due to the presence of an encrypted disk by using the dm-crypt mechanism (see "The Block-Level Encryption" section in Chapter 1).

In the above output we see several partitions; however, for a fully functional system, the needed ones are

- A *boot* partition, usually mounted on /boot, which holds the kernel images (we will see that actually it holds a special version of the kernel image: the fitimage).

- A *factory* partition, usually mounted on /factory, which holds critical information from the manufacturer (usually some system information and, possibly, a complete factory OS to be used to restore the system to a "factory condition").

- A *root* partition, usually mounted on /root, which holds the rootfs. As we saw in the previous section, this is an encrypted partition, and, in some circumstances (see the next two sections), it can be split into two (or more) partitions named root_a and root_b.

- A *data* partition, usually mounted on /data, which can hold backups and other useful information for the system, but with the main target of holding the updates data. In fact, during a system update, the new kernel and rootfs images are taken from this partition.

In the above list, the only encrypted partition is /root while other partitions are in plain text format. This is not a problem at all because in the boot and factory partitions all kernel and rootfs images are encrypted, while in /data we should be careful to encrypt all sensible files among the update binaries.

Well, now we can see in detail some possible secure boot implementation schemas, each with its pros and cons.

3.1 Rescue Schema

The factory schema is a way to boot the system, where we need a reliable way to restore the factory conditions. In this scenario, once the kernel starts, it loads the initramfs, and the init program will find the following partition scenario within the mass storage:

- One boot partition

- One factory partition

- One root partition

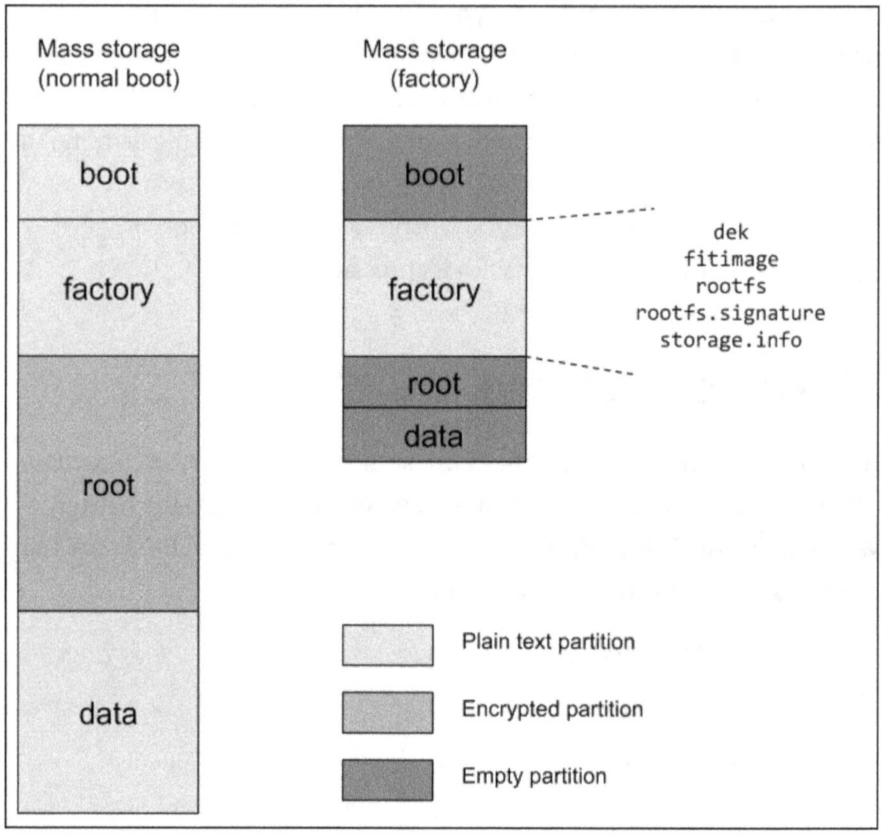

Figure 3-1. *A typical mass storage configuration for the rescue schema during the normal boot and factory-reset stage*

A practical example of this configuration is reported below:

```
# lsblk -o NAME,SIZE,TYPE,LABEL,MOUNTPOINTS /dev/mmcblk2
NAME             SIZE  TYPE  LABEL    MOUNTPOINTS
mmcblk2          14.6G disk
|-mmcblk2p1      128M  part  boot     /boot
|-mmcblk2p2      500M  part  factory  /factory
|-mmcblk2p3      3.9G  part
| `-root         3.9G  dm    root     /
`-mmcblk2p4      10G   part  data     /data
```

Within the boot partition (mounted on the same name directory), we have the following content:

```
# ls /boot/
fitimage   lost+found   rootfs.key.bb
```

where the fitimage file is the kernel with the DTB and the initramfs, while the file rootfs.key.bb holds the encryption key (in a wrapped form) used to decrypt the rootfs stored in the partition mmcblk0p3 (this key has been generated with the caam-keygen as described in the section "Using Vendor-Specific Key" in Chapter 1).

While in the factory partition (mounted on the same name directory), we have the following content:

```
# ls /factory/
dek            fitimage   rootfs      rootfs.signature
storage.info
```

This directory is built up during the factory production. The file fitimage (the kernel, DTB, and initramfs), while the two files named rootfs and rootfs.signature are obviously the factory rootfs (in an encrypted form) and its signature.

The storage.info file is a simple text file holding some system information, as shown below:

```
# cat /factory/storage.info
boot:1:8M:+128M:ext4
factory:0:0:+500M:ext4
root:0:0:+4000M:ext4
data:0:0:0:ext4
```

These data are used during a factory-reset to rebuild the system to its factory status.

For completeness, we can say that the above syntax means

- The first field is the partition's name (required).

- The second field is the partition's number (0 means it is up to the system).

- The third field is the partition's starting offset (0 means the end of the preceding partition).

- The fourth field is the partition's size (0 means to the end of the device).

- The fifth field is the filesystem type to be used on the partition.

A note on the dek file: this file holds the system's main encryption key but is vendor-specific. In fact, the above examples came from a secured system implemented on an iMX8-based machine, and this CPU series uses a special way to store the main encryption key: that is, a wrapped file, in this case.

Other systems just store this key in a protected area (usually some protected fuses), so on these systems this file is not present at all.

See the section "The Hybrid Approach" in Chapter 4 in order to see how this file can be generated.

Before ending this section, we should spend a few words to explain Figure 3-1. During normal functioning, the mass storage is partitioned as seen above and stated by the `storage.info` file; however, when the system has been built up into its factory, the mass storage can be reorganized in order to squeeze its image.

In fact, having a smaller image allows quicker initialization, since the data to be transferred into the mass storage is less; this permits reducing the per-piece production time.

Since all data in this stage are static, that is, exist in a *frozen* state, we can put all needed files for the factory production into the factory partition, leaving the other partition empty. This allows us to define some partitions smaller than what is reported in the `storage.info` file.

Altering a partition table is an easy task (we are going to use the `sgdisk` command to do it—see below), but if we want to do it without losing data, we must be careful not to move the placement of those partitions holding this data. In the rescue schema, all initial data are placed into the factory partition, while other partitions are empty; however, since boot is the first partition and we would rather not move data into the factory one, these two first partitions must be initially defined at their right size.

On the other hand, there are no problems if we define root and data partitions as small as possible. So, when the mass storage is initialized, the actual partitioning is something as reported below:

```
Device            Start       End Sectors  Size Type
/dev/loop9p1      16384    278527  262144  128M Linux filesystem
/dev/loop9p2     278528   1302527 1024000  500M Linux filesystem
/dev/loop9p3    1302528   1304575    2048    1M Linux filesystem
/dev/loop9p4    1304576   1306623    2048    1M Linux filesystem
```

The above lines are the output of the command `fdisk -l`, where we can see that the first two partitions (boot and factory) have their right sizes, while the other two (root and data) are just 1 MB in length.

Device names refer to the loop device `/dev/loop9` due to the fact we have used a loop device to get this information from instead of reading them directly on the target.

During the factory-reset, these two last partitions will be altered and defined to their final size (see the section "Doing a Factory-Reset" below, where we explain in detail these steps).

3.1.1 Doing a Normal Boot

In a normal boot, the bootloader (U-Boot) starts, and then it detects which is the actual boot partition:

```
...
Running bootcmd [normal] on mmc2...
switch to partitions #0, OK
mmc2(part 0) is current device
Schema: Rescue

...
```

Then it loads the fitimage file from it and then executes the kernel with the command line as reported by the kernel's boot messages shown below:

```
[    0.000000] Kernel command line: console=ttymxc1,115200
    device=/dev/mmcblk2 root=/dev/mmcblk2p3 rootwait rw
    initramfs_normal boot_schema=rescue root_name=root
[    0.000000] Unknown kernel command line parameters
    "initramfs_normal device=/dev/mmcblk2 boot_schema=rescue
    root_name=root", will be passed to user space.
```

The parameter that specifies to do a normal boot is `initramfs_normal`, while the `boot_schema` variable states that our system uses the rescue schema.

The U-Boot metacode that produces the output above will be presented below, split into several parts to better explain each step in detail.

We mention *U-Boot metacode* because we mean we are using a simplified version of real U-Boot scripting code to be more readable and to better understand what U-Boot really does.

Below are the initial settings:

```
schema=rescue
bootname=boot
rootname=root
image=fitimage
bootmode=normal
```

In this manner, by default, we are saying to U-Boot we wish to start a system in a normal boot (bootmode=normal), using the rescue schema (schema=rescue), and booting a kernel image named *fitimage* (image=fitimage), which is located in the boot partition (bootname=boot) that must mount as a root filesystem whatever is found in a partition named *root* (rootname=root).

Then the code continues as below, where we print some information, and we do some sanity checks:

```
...
echo Running bootcmd [${bootmode}] on mmc${mmcdev}...
mmc dev ${mmcdev}
echo -n "Schema: "
if test ${schema} = rescue ; then
        echo Rescue
```

```
elif test ${schema} = a_b ; then
        echo A/B [selector=${ab_selector}]
else
        panic "### PANIC ### Unknow booting schema '${schema}'"
fi
...
```

Note that the default booting mass storage device is addressed by the `mmcdev` variable; however, this may vary.

Now we should check the bootmode variable, and in the case of normal boot in the rescue schema, we essentially do nothing different from the default:

```
...
if test ${bootmode} = normal ; then
        if test ${schema} = a_b ; then
                ...
        fi;
elif test ${bootmode} = factory ; then
        ...
elif test ${bootmode} = update; then
        ...
else
        panic "### PANIC ### Unknown bootmode ${bootmode}"
fi
...
```

The code for the A/B schema has been removed for better readability; it will be readded in the section "Doing a Normal Boot" later in the chapter.

Now that all variables have been set, we should convert the `bootname` and `rootname` into their numeric counterparts:

```
...
part number mmc ${mmcdev} $bootname bootpart
part number mmc ${mmcdev} $rootname rootpart
...
```

In our case, we have that `bootpart` is 2 and `rootpart` is set to 3. So, as the last step, we have to properly set up the `bootargs` variable:

```
...
echo Booting from mmc ...; " \
setenv bootargs '... console=${console} \
    device=/dev/mmcblk${mmcdev} root=/dev/mmcblk${mmcdev}
    p${rootpart} \
    initramfs_${bootmode} boot_schema=${schema} root_
    name=${rootname}'
bootm ...
```

In this manner, the kernel command line has the following relevant settings (as already reported in the kernel messages above):

```
device=/dev/mmcblk2
root=/dev/mmcblk2p3
initramfs_normal
boot_schema=rescue
root_name=root
```

OK, now the kernel starts and executes the `/sbin/init` program in the initramfs, which in turn reads the encryption key from the `rootfs.key.bb` file and then mounts the encrypted rootfs via the `dm-crypt` mechanism.

Note that the kernel also passes to the user space other special parameters (`device`, `boot_schema`, and `root_name`) we can use to properly set up and run our applications.

A possible implementation of the code within the `init` program can be done with the following steps:

1) Mount the boot partition under the `/boot` directory, and load the root filesystem encryption key:

```
...
rootdev=$(get_cmdline_value root)
init=$(get_cmdline_value init)
schema=$(get_cmdline_value boot_schema)

mkdir_if_not_exist /boot
bootdev=$(get_device_by_label $device boot)
[ -z "$bootdev" ] && fatal "cannot detect boot
partition"

mount $bootdev /boot || fatal "cannot mount boot
partition"
caam-keygen import /boot/rootfs.key.bb rootfs.key || \
                fatal "cannot get rootfs's key!"
umount /boot
...
```

In this code, the get_device_by_label() function is used to detect which is the partition named *root* or *boot* and which is the booting schema used and a possible `init` program to execute instead of the default `/sbin/init` (see section "Fixing the Kernel

Command Line" in Appendix B for some security notes on this topic); once found, all names are stored within the corresponding variables, and the bootdev is used in the mount command to mount the partition under the /boot directory.

Now, by using the caam-keygen import command, we load the encryption key into the file /etc/caam/ rootfs.key (as described in the section "Using Vendor-Specific Key" in Chapter 1).

Note that this is a vendor-specific action; in fact, our CPU has the CAAM device, while another CPU may need to use a different approach, as, for example, a trusted key, as reported in the section "Using Trusted Key" in Chapter 1.

---

2) Store the root filesystem encryption key within the kernel keyring to be used with the device-mapper mechanism:

```
sh -c "keyctl new_session ; \
        keyctl padd logon logkey: @s < /etc/caam/
        rootfs.key ; \
dmsetup create root --table \"0 $(get_blockdev_size
${rootdev}) crypt capi:tk(cbc(aes))-plain :36:
logon:logkey: 0
${rootdev}0\""
dmsetup mknodes root
rootdev="/dev/mapper/root"
```

The command sequence supplied as a parameter for `sh -c` is just to avoid problems with the keys' access rights (see "The User Key" section in Chapter 1) and to automatically unlink the key when the session vanishes; also, the `dmsetup mknodes` command is to force the creation of the block device `/dev/mapper/root`, while the significant thing is the `dmsetup create root` command. This is the core of the root filesystem encryption!

The reader should note that, again, we have used a vendor-specific syntax since, for the CAAM, the key size is 36 bytes.

However, in the end, if everything goes well, the new root device is `/dev/mapper/root`, that's why the `rootdev` variable is set so.

3) Mount the encrypted root filesystem:

```
info "checking rootfs on $rootdev..."
fsck.ext4 -y $rootdev
info "mounting rootfs on $rootdev..."
mkdir -p $ROOT_DIR
wait_for_blockdev $rootdev || fatal "no
block device!"
mount $rootdev $ROOT_DIR || fatal "cannot
mount real rootfs!"
```

The call of the `fsck.ext4` command is used to check the root filesystem before mounting it (just in case some recoverable errors should be fixed up). Then we create a proper directory where to mount the root filesystem to be ready for the root switch (in our example, the variable ROOT_DIR is set to /mnt/root), and then we do the mount.

The `wait_for_blockdev` command function is just used to wait for the kernel to properly probe the block device where the root filesystem is stored. In fact, the kernel may need time to detect this device, and, at this point, it is not yet ready for mounting.

---

4)   Enter into the real root filesystem or hang in case of errors:

```
info "entering rootfs on $rootdev..."
move_mountpoint /dev /proc /sys /tmp
[ -f /etc/fw_env.config ] && \
        cp --parents /etc/fw_env.config $ROOT_DIR
if [ "$schema" == a_b ] ; then
        ...
fi
cp --parents /etc/rootfs.sign.key $ROOT_DIR
cp --parents /etc/caam/rootfs.key $ROOT_DIR
exec switch_root -c /dev/console $ROOT_DIR ${init:-/
sbin/init}

# Something goes wrong? Time to die...
fatal "System hangs!"
```

As seen in the section "Entering the Root Filesystem" in Chapter 2, the `switch_root` command is used to switch to another filesystem as the root of the mount tree, and with the command line below:

```
exec switch_root -c /dev/console $ROOT_DIR
${init:-/sbin/init}
```

we specify three important things:

1. The /dev/console device as console by using the -c option argument

2. The new root is the one addressed by the variable ROOT_DIR

3. The init process is the one addressed by the variable init, or /sbin/init if not defined

   Readers should note that we use the exec command to replace the current init process image with the new one.

   The move_mountpoint function is used to move the specified virtual filesystems on the new root before actually doing the swapping, while the final fatal function is needed to halt the system if everything goes wrong.

   OK, here are the steps needed to use an encrypted root filesystem; however, we have to spend a few words on the following lines of the last step:

```
if [ "$schema" == a_b ] ; then
        ...
fi
cp --parents /etc/rootfs.sign.key $ROOT_DIR
```

   Firstly, the cp command is used to save the root filesystem signature key; this is because, after the switch_root execution, this information will be lost, and we need it to be able to check the root filesystem during an update! This will be more clear in the section "Doing a System-Update" below.

Then the code removed from the `if` clause is specific for the A/B schema, and it will be explained in the dedicated section "Doing a Normal Boot" later in the chapter.

In order to show a functional example, below are reported the messages from our system during the rescue schema boot stage:

```
...
[    3.328646] Run /init as init process
init: factory_reset: subprocess 02-factory-reset.
sh not enabled! Skipped
init: system_update: subprocess 10-system-update.
sh not enabled! Skipped
[    3.445469] EXT4-fs (mmcblk2p1): mounted
filesystem 423db953-4c4d-43e 4-894d-038330336763
r/w with ordered data mode. Quota mode: none.
[    3.470190] EXT4-fs (mmcblk2p1): unmounting
filesystem 423db953-4c4d-43e4-894d-038330336763.
795247130
661245316
init: checking rootfs on /dev/mapper/root...
e2fsck 1.47.0 (5-Feb-2023)
root: clean, 22554/256000 files, 261472/1024000 blocks
init: mounting rootfs on /dev/mapper/root...
[    3.611417] EXT4-fs (dm-0): mounted filesystem
61a92dea-a1cf-4abf-97a2-442b065121c2 r/w with ordered
data mode. Quota mode: none.
...
[    4.148259] systemd[1]: Detected architecture arm64.
```

```
Welcome to BNDL Distro with XWayland 6.6-scarthgap
(scarthgap)!
...
```

After the init process has been started and the normal boot mode has been detected (the system skips the factory_reset and system_update procedures), it loads the encryption key into the keyring, and then the encrypted block device /dev/mapper/root is created, checked, and finally mounted as the real root filesystem. At this point, the system can do a normal boot by executing the main applications.

3.1.2 Doing a Factory-Reset

When we ask to do a factory-reset by setting bootmode=factory, U-Boot starts and it detects which is the actual factory partition:

```
...
Running bootcmd [factory] on mmc2...
switch to partitions #0, OK
mmc2(part 0) is current device
Schema: Rescue
...
```

The set bootmode=factory can be done in U-Boot in several ways: for example, by using a dedicated GPIO line, or directly via the serial console, or from a running system by using the fw_setenv utility (see man 8 fw_setenv—in Yocto the program should be held in the libubootenv-bin package).

Then it loads the fitimage file from it and then executes the kernel in it with the following command line:

```
...
[    0.000000] Kernel command line: console=ttymxc1,115200
device=/dev/m
mcblk2 root=/dev/mmcblk2p3 rootwait rw initramfs_factory boot_
schema=rescue root_name=root
[    0.000000] Unknown kernel command line parameters
"initramfs_factory device=/dev/mmcblk2 boot_schema=rescue root_
name=root", will be passed to user space.
...
```

The parameter that specifies to do a factory-reset boot is `initramfs_factory`, and now the U-Boot metacode looks like the following:

```
...
if test ${bootmode} = normal ; then
...
elif test ${bootmode} = factory ; then
        setenv bootname factory
        if test ${schema} = a_b ; then
            ...
        fi
elif test ${bootmode} = update; then
        ...
else
        panic "### PANIC ### Unknown bootmode ${bootmode}"
fi
part number mmc ${mmcdev} $bootname bootpart
part number mmc ${mmcdev} $rootname rootpart
...
```

Everything is quite similar to the normal boot, but now the `bootpart` variable points to `factory`. In this manner, we say to U-Boot: "Hey, do a boot using files into *factory* instead of files into the *boot* partition."

As above, the code relative to the A/B schema has been removed for better readability. It will be illustrated in the relative section below.

Again, the kernel starts and executes the `/sbin/init` program in the initramfs, which in turn reads the information within it and then properly sets up the boot and root partitions for the normal boot described above.

During this stage, the system generates the root filesystem encryption key, which is saved into the `rootfs.key.bb` file stored in the boot partition, and that will be used during all normal boots as explained in the previous section.

Note that the kernel also passes to the user space some parameters (`device`, `boot_schema`, and `root_name`) we can use to properly set up and run our applications according to the current booting conditions.

A possible implementation of the code within the `init` program can be done with the following steps:

1) Initialize some variables to be used later and move
   the GTP data to the end of the disk by using the
   `sgdisk` utility:

   ```
   ...
   local device=$(get_cmdline_value device)
   local schema=$(get_cmdline_value boot_schema)
   local root_name=$(get_cmdline_value root_name)
   local fit_label="fitimage"
   local factpath="/factory"

   sgdisk -e $device
   ...
   ```

This last step must be executed to properly set up the system's mass storage device with a valid partition table. Please keep in mind that the image we have created on the host machine doesn't have such information!

Variables `device`, `schema`, and `root_name` are extracted from the data passed by the kernel, so in this example they are set, respectively, as `/dev/mmcblk2`, `rescue`, and `root`.

2) Mount the factory partition under the `/factory` directory to be able to read basic system information (e.g., the `storage.info` file):

```
...
local factpart=$(get_device_by_label $device factory)
[ -z "$factpart" ] && \
        fatal "cannot detect factory partition"
info "mounting factory on $factpart..."
mkdir_if_not_exist /factory
mount -o ro $factpart /factory || \
                fatal "cannot read factory partition"

if [ "$schema" == a_b ] ; then
        ...
fi
...
```

Again, during this stage, we should do extra steps in the case our system is using the A/B schema; however, these aspects will be explained in detail in the dedicated section below.

3) Check if everything is in place and then verify the factory root filesystem signature:

```
...
[ -f "$factpath/fitimage" ] || fatal "no fitimage in
$factpath!"
[ -f "/factory/dek" ]          || warn "no DEK in /
factory!"
[ -f "$factpath/rootfs" ]    || fatal "no rootfs in
$factpath!"
[ -f "$factpath/rootfs.signature" ] || \
                fatal "no rootfs signature in
                $factpath!"

openssl dgst -verify /etc/rootfs.sign.key -sha256 \
        -signature $factpath/rootfs.signature \
        -binary $factpath/rootfs || \
                fatal "invalid rootfs signature"
...
```

Smart readers should have noticed that while the files `fitimage`, `rootfs`, and `rootfs.signature` are required to go further with the factory-reset procedure, the file `dek` is optional. This is an important note because, by doing so, we allow a successful factory-reset execution even on those systems that don't have this file, that is, on non-secured systems!

During the development, this behavior can be very useful since it allows developers to execute their code even on non-secured systems, but on the other hand, it can be a decrease in system security...

4) Reset the boot partition to the factory settings:

```
...
local bootdev=$(storage_info_get_device_by_label
$device boot)
local bootfstype=$(storage_info_get_fstype_by_
label boot)
info "repopulating boot on $bootdev [$bootfstype]..."
mkfs.${bootfstype} -q -F -L boot -I 256 $bootdev
mkdir_if_not_exist /boot
mount $bootdev /boot
cp $factpath/fitimage /boot/$fit_label || \
                        fatal "cannot copy $fit_label
                        in /boot"
[ -f /factory/dek ] && \
            cat /factory/dek >> /boot/$fit_label
...
```

First, we detect which is the mass storage device that
should hold the boot partition and the filesystem
type we should create on it, and then we use the
mkfs command to do the job. If everything goes
well, we can copy the fitimage file from the factory
partition to the boot one.

Note again that the dek file is managed apart; since we have decided
to consider it as optional, allowing a non-secured system to execute a
factory-reset procedure, we do an append to the fitimage only in the
case it is present (readers should note that in our example the dek
file is appended, but it will be managed differently on other systems).

Doing so, the factory-reset procedure prepares the boot partition for the normal boot by adding its fitimage to the boot partition.

5) Generate the root filesystem encryption key and save it into the boot partition:

```
...
info "generating rootfs private key..."
caam-keygen create rootfs.key ecb -s 16 || \
                        fatal "cannot generate rootfs
                        private key"
cp /etc/caam/rootfs.key.bb /boot/rootfs.key.bb || \
                        fatal "cannot add rootfs key!!"

umount /boot
...
```

As seen in "The Block-Level Encryption" section in Chapter 1, we generate the root filesystem encryption key for the CAAM (or whatever mechanism we can use for disk encryption), and then we save it into the boot partition.

When this step completes, we can safely unmount the boot partition.

6) Rebuild the partition table for the mass storage device, paying attention to not touch boot and factory partitions! This step is needed because we used the trick to get a smaller disk image as explained above, but now the time to build the real partition table has arrived, and the function `storage_info_rebuild_partition_table` is responsible for doing this job:

```
...
storage_info_rebuild_partition_table $device
...
```

7) Create the encrypted root filesystem and then
   repopulate it:

```
...
local rootdev=$(storage_info_get_device_by_label
$device $root_name)
local rootfstype=$(storage_info_get_fstype_by_
label $root_name)

info "formatting $root_name on $rootdev with
cipher..."
sh -c "keyctl new_session ; \
        keyctl padd logon logkey: @s < /etc/caam/
        rootfs.key ; \
        dmsetup create root --table \"0
        $(get_blockdev_size ${rootdev}) crypt
        capi:tk(cbc(aes))-plain :36:logon:logkey:
        0 ${rootdev}0\"" dmsetup mknodes root
        rootdev="/dev/mapper/root"

mkfs.${rootfstype} -q -F -L root -I 256 $rootdev
mkdir_if_not_exist /mnt
mount -t ${rootfstype} $rootdev /mnt
info "repopulating $root_name on $rootdev
[$rootfstype]..."
openssl enc -d -in $factpath/rootfs -aes-256-cbc \
            -K $(cat /etc/rootfs.key) \
            -iv $(cat /etc/rootfs.iv) | \
        tar xJf - -C /mnt || \
```

```
        fatal "cannot create rootfs partition"
...
```

This step is the core of the factory-reset procedure.

Once the root device has been detected (among the root filesystem type), we define the encrypted device by using `dmsetup` (this may vary for such devices that don't have the CAAM, they may use a trusted key). Note that the variable `rootdev` points to the real root device (i.e., the root partition) at the beginning, and then it points to the encrypted device (`/dev/mapper/root`) at the end.

Now we mount our new device under the `/mnt` directory, and we repopulate the root filesystem with all the needed files. Note that we supply to `openssl` the encryption key and the initial vectors instead of using a passphrase. This is because for the A/B schema we need this configuration to be able to securely save the encryption key (see the section "A/B Schema").

8) Wipe all partitions without touching:

- The factory partition, because it holds important system information

- The boot partition, because in a step above it has been populated with the needed files for the normal boot

- The root partition, because it has just been created

The function below does the job:

```
...
storage_info_wipe_partitions $device
...
```

In our example, the only affected partition by this
step is only data, but it may vary if we have other
partitions.

9) Finalizing the just recreated root filesystem:

```
...
info "finalizing the rootfs..."
storage_info_fix_fstab_entry $device /mnt

umount /factory
if [ "$schema" == a_b ] ; then
        ...
fi
umount /mnt
dmsetup remove root
...
```

Before the end, we must do some fixing and cleaning up.

Firstly, we should fix up the entries within the /etc/
fstab file; in fact, during the root filesystem building
up, the fstab file is usually generated as follows:

```
/dev/root                     /       auto defaults 1  1
proc                          /proc   proc defaults 0  0
...
/dev/disk/by-label/boot     /boot   auto noatime 0  0
/dev/disk/by-label/factory /factory auto ro      0  0
/dev/disk/by-label/data     /data   auto noatime 0  2
```

But using labels to point to partitions may be error-prone, so we prefer to replace each label with the unique partition UUID value as follows:

```
/dev/root                                         /         auto  ...
proc                                              /proc     proc  ...
...
UUID="423db953-4c4d-43e4-894d-038330336763" /boot     auto  ...
UUID="3d3575ac-378e-420a-bb21-10043a692501" /factory  auto  ...
UUID="949820ce-e177-415c-9369-0ceb1eaeaf26" /data     auto  ...
```

Warning   In the above output, each line has been truncated due to space reasons.

The function `storage_info_fix_fstab_entry` does the above job.

Then we can safely unmount the factory partition and the temporary root filesystem from the `/mnt` directory and then remove the mapped block device. This last step is needed because, when the updating is ended, the system will continue doing a normal boot, which in turn will remount the root filesystem as explained above.

Again, in the case of the A/B schema, the procedure will do some extra steps, which will be explained in the section "Doing a Factory-Reset" later in the chapter.

10)   At this point the update is almost finished; the only remaining thing to do is to notify the bootloader that the next boot must be done as a normal boot:

```
...
bundle-set-bootmode.sh normal
info "done!"
```

In the above example, the script `bundle-set-bootmode.sh` is used to write into the bootloader's environment.

In order to show a functional example, below are reported the messages from our system during the factory-reset procedure for the rescue schema.

Since the output below is quite long, we have broken it up into several pieces to be able to explain each step as soon as they appear in the listing.

The init process starts, and a factory-reset request has been detected:

```
...
[    4.107226] Run /init as init process
[    5.178438]  mmcblk2: p1 p2 p3 p4
The operation has completed successfully.
init: factory_reset: mounting factory on /dev/mmcblk2p2...
[    5.220900] EXT4-fs (mmcblk2p2): mounted filesystem
3d3575ac-378e-420 a-bb21-10043a692501 ro with ordered data
mode. Quota mode: none.
...
```

The factory partition has been mounted, so we can go further and build up the boot partition:

```
...
Verified OK
```

```
init: factory_reset: repopulating boot on /dev/mmcblk2p1
[ext4]...
[    6.549019] EXT4-fs (mmcblk2p1): mounted filesystem
423db953-4c4d-43e 4-894d-038330336763 r/w with ordered data
mode. Quota mode: none.
init: factory_reset: generating rootfs private key...
[    8.574019] EXT4-fs (mmcblk2p1): unmounting filesystem 423db
953-4c4d-43e4-894d-038330336763.
```

...

When the boot partition has been created and the root filesystem encryption key has been added, then the boot partition can be safely unmounted. Then we go further in rebuilding the partition table for the current mass storage device (/dev/mmcblk2 in our example):

...

```
init: factory_reset: deleting partition #3 root on /dev/
mmcblk2...
Warning: The kernel is still using the old partition table.
The new table will be used at the next reboot or after you
run partprobe(8) or kpartx(8)
The operation has completed successfully.
init: factory_reset: deleting partition #4 data on /dev/
mmcblk2...
Warning: The kernel is still using the old partition table.
The new table will be used at the next reboot or after you
run partprobe(8) or kpartx(8)
The operation has completed successfully.
init: factory_reset: creating partition #3 root
[ext4@0:+4000M]...
Warning: The kernel is still using the old partition table.
The new table will be used at the next reboot or after you
```

```
run partprobe(8) or kpartx(8)
The operation has completed successfully.
init: factory_reset: creating partition #4 data [ext4@0:0]...
Warning: The kernel is still using the old partition table.
The new table will be used at the next reboot or after you
run partprobe(8) or kpartx(8)
The operation has completed successfully.
...
```

Now the encrypted root filesystem must be formatted and then repopulated:

```
...
init: factory_reset: formatting root on /dev/mmcblk2p3 with
cipher...
637478479
111261603
[   14.557174] EXT4-fs (dm-0): mounted filesystem 61a92dea-
a1cf-4abf-97a2-442b065121c2 r/w with ordered data mode. Quota
mode: none.
init: factory_reset: repopulating root on /dev/mapper/root
[ext4]...
...
```

Once the root filesystem is ready, we can do some minor jobs:

```
...
init: factory_reset: resizing partition #4 data...
init: factory_reset: wiping partition data on /dev/mmcblk2p4
[ext4]...
...
```

As requested by the file `storage.info`, the data partition must be resized until the end of the mass storage device (see the section "Rescue Schema" above where we explained the meaning of `storage.info` fields). After the resizing, the data partition is also wiped.

Then, as the last step, all requested resources for the factory-reset, and no more needed, are released:

```
...
init: factory_reset: finalizing the rootfs...
[   72.168253] EXT4-fs (mmcblk2p2): unmounting filesystem
3d3575ac-378e-420a-bb21-10043a692501.
[   77.496446] EXT4-fs (dm-0): unmounting filesystem 61a92dea-
a1cf-4abf-97a2-442b065121c2.
init: factory_reset: done!
...
```

Now the factory-update is finished, and the system can do a normal boot:

```
...
init: system_update: subprocess 10-system-update.sh not
enabled! Skipped
[   77.654069] EXT4-fs (mmcblk2p1): mounted filesystem
423db953-4c4d-43e 4-894d-038330336763 r/w with ordered data
mode. Quota mode: none.
[   77.678611] EXT4-fs (mmcblk2p1): unmounting filesystem 423db
953-4c4d-43e4-894d-038330336763.
1045733860
12428042
init: checking rootfs on /dev/mapper/root...
e2fsck 1.47.0 (5-Feb-2023)
root: clean, 22517/256000 files, 261329/1024000 blocks
init: mounting rootfs on /dev/mapper/root...
```

```
[   77.812900] EXT4-fs (dm-0): mounted filesystem 61a92dea-
a1cf-4abf-97a2-442b065121c2 r/w with ordered data mode. Quota
mode: none.
init: entering rootfs on /dev/mapper/root...
...
[   78.351867] systemd[1]: Detected architecture arm64.

Welcome to BNDL Distro with XWayland 6.6-scarthgap (scarthgap)!
...
```

If we recall what showed in the preceding section "Doing a Normal Boot," we can verify that a normal boot is actually executed.

3.1.3 Doing a System-Update

When we ask to do a system-update by setting bootmode=update, U-Boot starts and the messages change as below:

```
...
Running bootcmd [update] on mmc2...
switch to partitions #0, OK
mmc2(part 0) is current device
Schema: Rescue
...
```

U-Boot starts, tries to locate the directory where the updating files are located, loads the fitimage file from it, and then executes the kernel in it with the following command line:

```
...
[    0.000000] Kernel command line: console=ttymxc1,115200
device=/dev/mmcblk2 root=/dev/mmcblk2p3 rootwait rw initramfs_
update boot_schema=rescue root_name=root
```

```
[    0.000000] Unknown kernel command line parameters
"initramfs_update device=/dev/mmcblk2 boot_schema=rescue root_
name=root", will be passed to user space.
...
```

The parameter that specifies to do a normal boot is initramfs_update, and now the U-Boot metacode that implements these steps looks like the following:

```
...
if test ${bootmode} = normal ; then
        ...
elif test ${bootmode} = factory ; then
        ...
elif test ${bootmode} = update; then
        setenv bootname data
        setenv image update/fitimage
        if test ${schema} = a_b ; then
                panic "### PANIC ### Cannot update (A/B
                schema)!"
        fi
else
        panic "### PANIC ### Unknown bootmode ${bootmode}"
fi
part number mmc ${mmcdev} $bootname bootpart
part number mmc ${mmcdev} $rootname rootpart
...
```

Now bootname points to the data partition, and the image file is set to update/fitimage; this means that U-Boot now expects to find a valid fitimage file under the directory /data/update (as explained below).

Note that this is merely a convention; we can use a different directory, of course. However, what is crucial is that both U-Boot and user space agree on the same location!

Note also that this boot mode is invalid in the case of an A/B schema. In fact, as we will see later in this book, the system-update procedure for this schema is done completely in user space.

In this scenario, the kernel starts and executes the `/sbin/init` program in the initramfs (which is already the updated version), which in turn reads the information within it and then properly updates the files within the boot partition and updates all files into the root (note that, in this case, a backup of some configuration files or data could be required—see below).

Due to all the above considerations, it's obvious that this time, both preliminary and later steps are needed before starting the real update. In fact, the user must provide the updating files before starting the update, and they should also consider saving important files that must be present in the updated system!

Let's see how we can solve these issues.

Regarding the update files, in our example, they are stored in a file named `root-image_imx8mp-icore_v0.90.bundle` which is located in the `/data` directory.

Note that where the update file is located is not relevant; what is significant is where the update files will be placed, and to do this job, a proper tool is the one reported below:

```
# bundle-update.sh /data/root-image_imx8mp-icore_v0.90.bundle
bundle-update.sh: extracting bundle file in /data/update...
bundle-update.sh: bootmode is now set to "update". So, just
reboot to do the updating!
```

By default in our example, all update files are stored under the /data/ update directory, which looks like the following:

```
# ls -l /data/update/
total 254288
-rw-r--r-- 1 root root        256 Mar  5  2025 root-image-
imx8mp-icore.rootfs.tar.xz.signature
-rw-r--r-- 1 root root 185674448 Mar  5  2025 root-image-
imx8mp-icore.rootfs.tar.xz.signed.bin
lrwxrwxrwx 1 root root         42 Mar  5  2025 fitimage ->
fitimage-imx8mp-icore.bin.signed.bin
-rw-r--r-- 1 root root  74707032 Mar  5  2025 fitimage-imx8mp-
icore.bin.signed.bin
lrwxrwxrwx 1 root root         59 Mar  5  2025 rootfs -> root-
image-imx8mp-icore.rootfs.tar.xz.signed.bin
lrwxrwxrwx 1 root root         58 Mar  5  2025 rootfs.signature
-> root-image-imx8mp-icore.rootfs.tar.xz.signature
```

Apart from the symbolic links, all files are the same as we can find in the factory directory, that is, the fitimage (the kernel with the embedded initramfs and the device tree file) and the root filesystem archive with its signature.

Note that the dek file is not present because it has been appended to the fitimage by the `bundle-update.sh` (as shown below). However, this is a vendor-specific case, since for systems that don't use it, the `/data/update` directory will look like the above by default.

A possible implementation of the core of the bundle-update.sh is shown below:

```
...
UPDATE_DIR="/data/update"
...
[ $# -lt 1 ] && usage
blob=$1
dir=$UPDATE_DIR
[ $# -ge 2 ] && dir=$2
...
if [ $schema == a_b ] ; then
        ...
else
        if [ ! -e $dir ] ; then
                mkdir $dir || fatal "cannot create
                directory $dir"
        fi
        [ -d $dir ] || fatal "invalid target directory $dir"

        # Get fitimage and roots images from the bundle archive
        info "extracting bundle file in $dir..."
        blob_extract_and_link $blob $BUNDLE_FIT_IMG $dir
        fitimage
        if [ $BUNDLE_KIND == "secured" ] ; then
                cat /factory/dek >> $dir/fitimage || \
                        fatal "cannot append dek file to
                        fitimage"
        fi
        blob_extract_and_rename $blob $BUNDLE_ROOTFS_IMG \
                                        $dir rootfs
        blob_extract_and_rename $blob $BUNDLE_ROOTFS_SIGN \
```

```
                                        $dir rootfs.
                                        signature

        fw_setenv bootmode "update" || fatal "cannot set the
        bootmode!"
        info "bootmode set to \"update\". Reboot to complete
        the update"
fi

exit 0
```

Again, the code for the A/B schema has been removed for better readability, and it will be explained in detail in the dedicated section below.

However, here it can be a security risk! In fact, in this example, if an attacker gives us an invalid update bundle, we may try to install it, causing a system hang due to the fact the system cannot load the fitimage! In this situation, we can recover by instructing the bootloader in such a way that it tries to do a normal boot in this situation; also, we should check both fitimage and root filesystem signatures before installing them (this is just another reason why every sensible file should be encrypted and then signed, rather than the inverse!).

The task of the above tool is just to prepare the /data/update directory with all needed files to do a proper boot with these new files. In fact, it's simple to see how it works: the UPDATE_DIR variable is initialized with the well-known /data/update/ pathname, and once we supply the file where updates rely, it uses the blob_extract_and_link function to properly install these files. As a last step, it notifies the bootloader to execute the system-update procedure at the next boot by setting bootmode to the update value.

Now, during a successive system boot, the bootloader loads the new `fitimage` (as explained above), and then the system-update procedure begins. A possible implementation of the code within the `init` program can be done with the following steps:

1) Set some variables to their default:

```
...
local device=$(get_cmdline_value device)
local UPDATE_DIR="/data/update"
...
```

2) Then we set the bootmode variable to *normal-boot*. This is because, in case of error, we can just restart the system to do a normal boot and recover the situation:

```
...
bundle-set-bootmode.sh normal
...
```

3) Then we try to mount the factory partition under the same name directory:

```
...
local factpart=$(get_device_by_label $device factory)
[ -z "$factpart" ] && \
        fatal "cannot detect factory partition"

info "mounting factory on $factpart..."
mkdir_if_not_exist /factory
mount -o ro $factpart /factory || \
        fatal "cannot read factory partition"
...
```

Note that, in case of error, we hang the system by using the `fatal`
command. This is not mandatory, and we can simply do a reboot
(by using the `restart` command as below), but we prefer to do
it because not being able to mount the factory directory is not just
a *normal* error; it's a big problem! In fact, that directory holds vital
system information we need to do an update or even a factory-reset.

4) Then we try to mount the data partition under the
    same name directory and then verify that the update
    directory exists:

```
...
local datadev=$(storage_info_get_device_by_label
$device data)
local datafstype=$(storage_info_get_fstype_by_
label data)
info "looking for update directory on $datadev
[$datafstype]..."
mkdir_if_not_exist /data
mount -o ro $datadev /data || \
        restart "cannot mount data partition"
[ -d $UPDATE_DIR ] || \
        restart "no $UPDATE directory! Abort"
...
```

5) Once the /data/update path is available, we can go
    further and check if everything is in place:

```
...
[ -f "$UPDATE_DIR/fitimage" ] || \
        restart "no fitimage in $UPDATE_DIR!"
```

```
[ -f "/factory/dek" ] || warn "no DEK in /factory!"
[ -f "$UPDATE_DIR/rootfs" ] || \
        restart "no rootfs in $UPDATE_DIR!"
[ -f "$UPDATE_DIR/rootfs.signature" ] || \
        restart "no rootfs signature in $UPDATE_DIR!"
...
```

**Even in this case, the missing dek file is not considered a fatal error
to be able to execute even non-secured images.**

---

6) Then we must check the root filesystem signature
   before installation:

   ```
   ...
   openssl dgst -verify /etc/rootfs.sign.key -sha256 \
           -signature $UPDATE_DIR/rootfs.signature \
           -binary $UPDATE_DIR/rootfs || \
                   restart "invalid rootfs signature"
   ...
   ```

7) Now we enter into a critical zone. In fact, after this point
   we cannot do a simple reset to recover the system! The
   update procedure **must** go on, or the system will break
   (this is the classical situation when we do an update on
   a consumer device and we get the message: System is
   updating. **Please do not power off**).

   In this scenario, we must be sure that a factory reset
   is done on the next reboot if the procedure doesn't
   end properly:

   ```
   ...
   bundle-set-bootmode.sh factory
   ```

...

Then we rebuild the boot partition adding the new
`fitimage` (and dek) file:

```
...
local bootdev=$(storage_info_get_device_by_label
$device boot)
local bootfstype=$(storage_info_get_fstype_by_
label boot)
info "repopulating boot on $bootdev [$bootfstype]..."
mkfs.${bootfstype} -q -F -L boot -I 256 $bootdev
mkdir_if_not_exist /boot
mount $bootdev /boot || fatal "cannot mount boot
partition"
cp $UPDATE_DIR/fitimage /boot/fitimage
[ -f /factory/dek ] && \
        cat /factory/dek >> /boot/fitimage
...
```

8) Then we generate a new encryption key for the root
    filesystem in the same manner as we did during the
    factory-reset, saving the `rootfs.key.bb` file in the
    boot partition:

```
...
info "generating rootfs private key..."
caam-keygen create rootfs.key ecb -s 16 || \
                fatal "cannot generate rootfs
                private key"
cp /etc/caam/rootfs.key.bb /boot/rootfs.key.bb || \
                fatal "cannot add rootfs key!"
...
```

As for the factory-reset, we underline the fact that this step is vendor-specific, and it can be replaced by using a trusted key.

9) Now the boot partition has been recreated, so we can safely unmount it:

```
...
umount /boot
rmdir /boot
...
```

10) The next step is rebuilding the root filesystem into its encrypted partition as usual, but using the updating files:

```
...
local rootdev=$(storage_info_get_device_by_label
$device root)
local rootfstype=$(storage_info_get_fstype_by_
label root)

info "formatting $rootdev with cipher..."
sh -c "keyctl new_session ; \
        keyctl padd logon logkey: @s < /etc/caam/
        rootfs.key ; \
        dmsetup create root --table \"0 $(get_blockdev_
        size ${rootdev}) crypt capi:tk(cbc(aes))-plain
        :36:logon:logkey: 0 $rootdev 0\
""

dmsetup mknodes root
rootdev="/dev/mapper/root"
mkfs.${rootfstype} -q -F -L root -I 256 $rootdev
mkdir_if_not_exist /mnt
```

```
mount -t ${rootfstype} $rootdev /mnt
info "repopulating root on $rootdev [$rootfstype]..."
openssl enc -d -in $UPDATE_DIR/rootfs -aes-256-cbc \
                -K $(cat /etc/rootfs.key) \
                -iv $(cat /etc/rootfs.iv) | \
        tar xJf - -C /mnt || \
                fatal "cannot create rootfs partition"
...
```

11) Now, the update is quite ended, so we can unmount
the data partition:

```
...
umount /data
rmdir /data
...
```

12) And, as per the factory-update, we fix up the /
etc/fstab file (see step 9 in the preceding section
"Doing a Factory-Reset"):

```
...
info "finalizing the rootfs..."
storage_info_fix_fstab_entry $device /mnt
...
```

13) Now we can safely unmount the factory partition
and the temporary rootfs, then we remove the
mapped block device, and, as a last step, we must
notify the bootloader that now it can safely redo a
normal boot:

```
...
umount /factory
umount /mnt
```

```
dmsetup remove root

bundle-set-bootmode.sh normal

info "done!"
```

In order to show a functional example, let's see the steps needed to properly do a system-update.

Firstly, we must install all needed updating files with the `bundle-update.sh` tool:

```
$ bundle-update.sh /data/root-image-imx8mp-icore_v0.90.bundle
bundle-update.sh: extracting bundle file in /data/update...
bundle-update.sh: bootmode set to "update". Reboot to complete
the update
```

Then we can consider backing up some important files to be able to reinstall them when the updating is finished.

Note that this step is not needed if no special settings have been done within the root partition.

To do so, we have a dedicated tool:

```
$ bundle-backup.sh -L create
bundle-backup.sh: stopping service systemd-networkd.service...
Stopping 'systemd-networkd.service', but its triggering units
are still active:
systemd-networkd.socket
bundle-backup.sh: creating /data/imx8mp-icore-20250305194125.
backup from files list /etc/bundle/backup.conf
etc/systemd/network/50-eth0.network
etc/ssh/
etc/ssh/moduli
```

```
etc/ssh/ssh_host_ecdsa_key.pub
etc/ssh/sshd_config
...
etc/ssh/ssh_config
bundle-backup.sh: setting "latest" link to /data/backup/imx8mp-
icore-202 50305194125.backup...
bundle-backup.sh: setting "restore_after_update" link to /data/
backup/imx8mp-icore-20250305194125.backup...
bundle-backup.sh: starting service systemd-networkd.service...
bundle-backup.sh: done
```

This tool is elementary: it reads a file list to be backed up from the file `/etc/bundle/backup.conf` and creates an archive under the `/data/backup/` directory. Note that, since the system-update procedure doesn't touch the data partition, these files can be restored once the update is finished.

By using the `-L` option argument, we notify the tool to create a symbolic link named `latest` into the backup directory, which will be used by a proper service to restore all backed up files (see the example below).

OK, now we can safely do a reboot, and the system booting messages should look like as reported below:

```
...
[    3.411674] Run /init as init process
init: factory_reset: subprocess 02-factory-reset.sh not
enabled! Skipped
init: resize_partitions: subprocess 05-resize-partitions.sh not
enabled! Skipped
init: system_update: mounting factory on /dev/mmcblk2p2...
...
```

Here a system-update request has been detected, and the procedure starts.

```
...
[    3.552387] EXT4-fs (mmcblk2p2): mounted filesystem
3d3575ac-378e-420 a-bb21-10043a692501 ro with ordered data
mode. Quota mode: none.
init: system_update: looking for update directory on /dev/
mmcblk2p4 [ext4]...
[    3.646031] EXT4-fs (mmcblk2p4): orphan cleanup on
readonly fs
[    3.654263] EXT4-fs (mmcblk2p4): mounted filesystem
207ffdb7-9686-4f1
e-b240-db5404bcdfe9 ro with ordered data mode. Quota
mode: none.
Verified OK
...
```

The update file's signature has been verified, and then the boot partition is repopulated with the new fitimage (and other) file:

```
...
init: system_update: repopulating boot on /dev/mmcblk2p1
[ext4]...
/dev/mmcblk2p1 contains a ext4 file system labelled 'boot'
        last mounted on /boot on Wed Mar  5 15:13:32 2025
[    4.676448] EXT4-fs (mmcblk2p1): mounted filesystem
43c03375-7b37-418 a-8cf3-220767455e0c r/w with ordered data
mode. Quota mode: none.
...
```

Then a new root filesystem key is generated and the root partition is repopulated:

```
...
init: system_update: generating rootfs private key...
[    6.779482] EXT4-fs (mmcblk2p1): unmounting filesystem
43c03375-7b37-418a-8cf3-220767455e0c.
init: system_update: formatting /dev/mmcblk2p3 with cipher...
1048667175
324543032
[    8.652250] EXT4-fs (dm-0): mounted filesystem
5f4de69e-4f22-4969-977f-ca190e5ef660 r/w with ordered data
mode. Quota mode: none.
init: system_update: repopulating root on /dev/mapper/root
[ext4]...
[   57.825977] EXT4-fs (mmcblk2p4): unmounting filesystem
207ffdb7-9686-4f1e-b240-db5404bcdfe9.
init: system_update: finalizing the rootfs...
[   59.089106] EXT4-fs (mmcblk2p2): unmounting filesystem
3d3575ac-378e-420a-bb21-10043a692501.
[   64.338410] EXT4-fs (dm-0): unmounting filesystem
5f4de69e-4f22-4969-977f-ca190e5ef660.
init: system_update: done!
...
```

Great! The system-update procedure is now finished, and a normal boot, with the new files, can begin:

```
...
[   64.444400] EXT4-fs (mmcblk2p1): mounted filesystem
43c03375-7b37-418a-8cf3-220767455e0c r/w with ordered data
mode. Quota mode: none.
```

```
[   64.469375] EXT4-fs (mmcblk2p1): unmounting filesystem
43c03375-7b37-418a-8cf3-220767455e0c.
498901129
284519802
init: checking rootfs on /dev/mapper/root...
e2fsck 1.47.0 (5-Feb-2023)
root: clean, 22517/256000 files, 261328/1024000 blocks
init: mounting rootfs on /dev/mapper/root...
[   64.606252] EXT4-fs (dm-0): mounted filesystem
5f4de69e-4f22-4969-977f-ca190e5ef660 r/w with ordered data
mode. Quota mode: none.
init: entering rootfs on /dev/mapper/root...
...
[   65.148090] systemd[1]: Detected architecture arm64.

Welcome to BNDL Distro with XWayland 6.6-scarthgap (scarthgap)!
...
```

Keep looking at the booting messages, we also see the following message:

```
...
        Starting Bundle backup restore...
...
```

This is the restore service we talked about above that is responsible for restoring the latest backup (i.e., the one obtained with the -L option argument for the bundle-backup.sh command above).

To see that everything has really gone well, we can use the systemctl command as reported below:

```
$ systemctl status -l --no-pager bundle-backup
* bundle-backup.service - Bundle backup restore
```

```
    Loaded: loaded (8;;file://imx8mp-icore-devel/usr/lib/
    systemd/
system/bundle-backup.service/usr/lib/systemd/system/bundle-
backup.service8;;; enabled; preset: enabled)
    Active: active (exited) since Wed 2025-03-05 15:13:37 UTC;
    1min 59s ago
   Process: 499 ExecStart=/usr/sbin/bundle-backup.sh restore
   --link-restore (code=exited, status=0/SUCCESS)
   Process: 616 ExecStartPost=rm /data/backup/restore_after_
   update (code=exited, status=0/SUCCESS)
  Main PID: 499 (code=exited, status=0/SUCCESS)
       CPU: 223ms

...
Mar 05 15:13:36 imx8mp-icore-devel bundle-backup.sh[499]:
bundle-backup.
sh: starting service systemd-networkd.service...
Mar 05 15:13:37 imx8mp-icore-devel bundle-backup.sh[499]:
bundle-backup.
sh: done
Mar 05 15:13:37 imx8mp-icore-devel bundle-backup.sh[499]:
Mar 05 15:13:37 imx8mp-icore-devel systemd[1]: Finished Bundle
backup restore.
```

At this point, we can easily verify that the system has been updated as requested.

3.2 A/B Schema

The A/B schema is a way to boot the system from two partitions alternatively. In this manner, we can update the system while it is running.

In fact, as already seen, in the rescue schema, to update the system, we have to reboot it, then wait until the end of the update, and in the end, we can launch the new release. All these steps are done at the same time during a single booting sequence, and the installation stage can take many minutes to complete, according to the rootfs size and the CPU speed.

On the other hand, by using the A/B schema, we can do a complete update while the current application release is up and running (which can be very useful when we need to have an always-up system). This behavior is really useful when our system cannot stop its functioning, not even to update itself!

In this scenario, once the kernel starts, it loads the initramfs, and then the `init` program will find the following partition scenario within the mass storage:

- One `boot` partition

- One `factory` partition

- `root_a` and `root_b` partitions

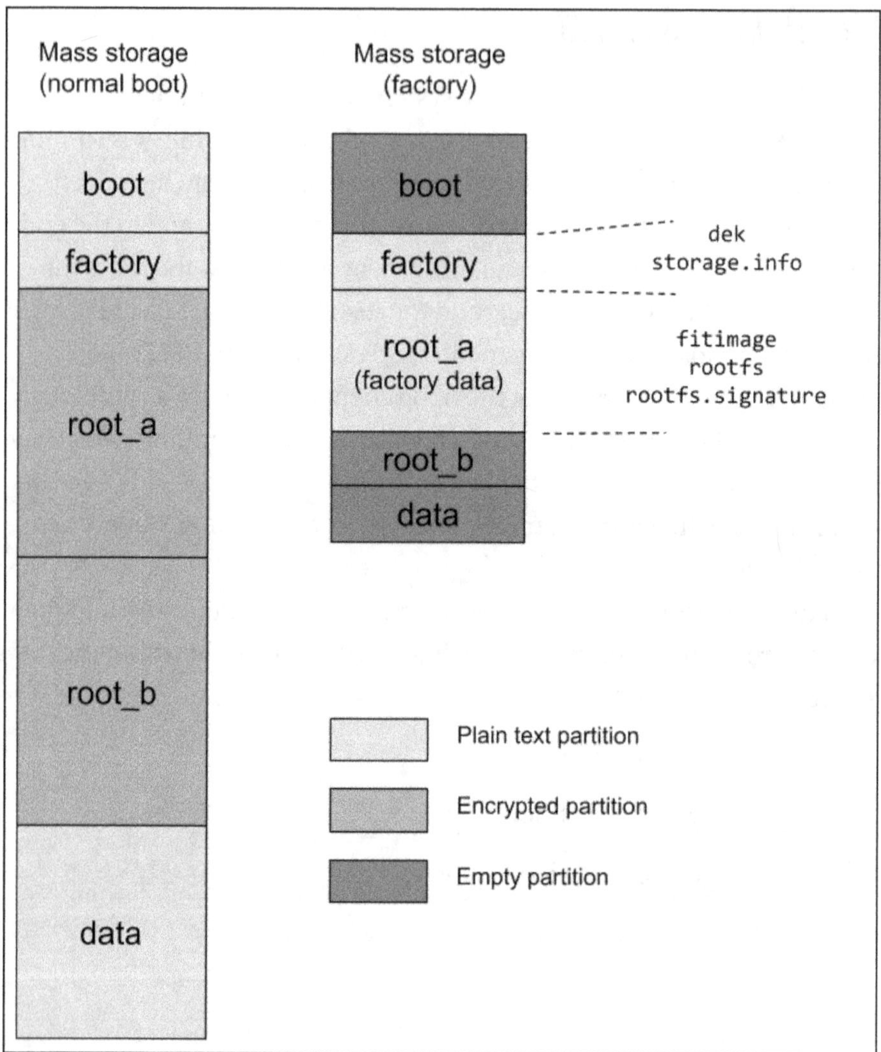

Figure 3-2. *A typical mass storage configuration for the A/B schema during the normal boot and factory-reset stage*

A practical example of this configuration is reported below:

```
# lsblk -o NAME,SIZE,TYPE,LABEL,MOUNTPOINTS /dev/mmcblk2
NAME             SIZE TYPE LABEL    MOUNTPOINTS
mmcblk2         14.6G disk
|-mmcblk2p1     256M part boot     /boot
|-mmcblk2p2       8M part factory /factory
|-mmcblk2p3     3.9G part root_a
|-mmcblk2p4     3.9G part root_b
| `-root        3.9G dm   root     /
`-mmcblk2p5     6.5G part data     /data
```

Compared to the rescue schema, we can notice that the factory partition can be tiny (in the above example, it is just 8 MB instead of the 500 MB needed for the rescue counterpart), while the size needed for the root filesystem is doubled! So, it's quite common to adopt larger mass storage devices to support this scenario.

Within the boot partition (mounted on the same name directory), we have the following content:

```
# ls /boot/
fitimage_a  fitimage_b  lost+found  rootfs.key.bb
```

where the `fitimage_a` and `fitimage_b` files are the kernel with the DTB and the initrmafs, respectively, for the A and B sections, while the file `rootfs.key.bb` holds the encryption key (in a wrapped form) used to decrypt both the root filesystem stored in the partitions `mmcblk0p3` and `mmcblk0p4`.

Note that the above output is from a system that has been updated at least once; in fact, during the first normal boot after the factory-reset, when no system-update procedures have been executed yet, the `fitimage_a` file is not present.

While in the factory partition (mounted on the same name) directory, we have the following content:

```
# ls /factory/
dek  lost+found  storage.info
```

Now the factory fitimage and its credentials are gone, while the storage.info and dek files are again, the former, a file holding some system's information, and the latter, the file holding the system's main encryption key (as per the rescue schema—see the preceding section "Doing a Normal Boot").

The storage.info file now has the following content:

```
# cat /factory/storage.info
boot:1:8M:+256M:ext4
factory:0:0:+8M:ext4
root_a:0:0:+4000M:ext4
root_b:0:0:+4000M:ext4
data:0:0:0:ext4
```

The meaning of each field is the same as for the rescue schema (see the section "Rescue Schema") and now we can easily see that the factory partition has been reduced to a few megabytes, while the mass storage usage is increased due to the fact of the two root filesystem images.

As per the rescue schema, the factory partitioning has been reworked to occupy as little mass memory as possible. This time the root filesystem archive has been placed into the *root_a* partition, so during the factory reset the initial system will be installed into the *root_b* partition, and the *root_a* partition will be filled during the first system-update. So, when the mass storage is initialized, the actual partitioning is something as reported below:

```
Device            Start       End Sectors   Size Type
/dev/loop9p1      16384    540671  524288   256M Linux filesystem
/dev/loop9p2     540672    557055   16384     8M Linux filesystem
/dev/loop9p3     557056   1171455  614400   300M Linux filesystem
/dev/loop9p4    1171456   1173503    2048     1M Linux filesystem
/dev/loop9p5    1173504   1175551    2048     1M Linux filesystem
```

The above lines are the output of the command `fdisk -l`, where we can see that the boot partition has been doubled since now it holds two fitimage files, the *factory* partition is a few megabytes, and the *root_a* partition is large enough to hold the factory root filesystem archive. Then other partitions (*root_b* and *data*) are just 1 MB in length.

As above, device names refer to the loop device `/dev/loop9` instead of the real mass storage device of the target.

During the factory-reset, these the *root_a*, *root_b* and *data* partitions will be altered and defined to their final size (see the section "Doing a Factory-Reset" below, where we explain in detail these steps). The important note here is that the *root_a* partition must be enlarged only and not moved! Or the data it holds can be lost before we can install our new system.

3.2.1 Doing a Normal Boot

In a normal boot, the bootloader (U-Boot) starts, and then it detects which is the actual boot partition:

```
...
Running bootcmd [normal] on mmc2...
switch to partitions #0, OK
```

```
mmc2(part 0) is current device
Schema: A/B [selector=b]
...
```

Then it loads the `fitimage_b` file from it and then executes the kernel with the command line as reported by the kernel's boot messages shown below:

```
...
[    0.000000] Kernel command line: console=ttymxc1,115200
device=/dev/mmcblk2 root=/dev/mmcblk2p4 rootwait rw initramfs_
normal boot_schema=a_b
root_name=root_b
[    0.000000] Unknown kernel command line parameters
"initramfs_normal device=/dev/mmcblk2 boot_schema=a_b root_
name=root_b", will be passed to user space.
...
```

The parameter that specifies to do a normal boot is `initramfs_normal`, while the `boot_schema` variable states that our system uses the A/B schema.

As done for the rescue schema above, we are going to use again the U-Boot metacode to explain the steps that produce the above output.

This time the initial settings are the following:

```
schema=a_b
ab_selector=b
bootname=boot
rootname=root
image=fitimage
bootmode=normal
```

However, now we are using the A/B schema, so variables `image` and `rootname` are redefined as shown below:

```
...
if test ${bootmode} = normal ; then
        if test ${schema} = a_b ; then
                setenv image fitimage_${ab_selector}
                setenv rootname root_${ab_selector}
        fi;
elif test ${bootmode} = factory ; then
        ...
elif test ${bootmode} = update; then
        ...
else
        panic \"### PANIC ### Unknow bootmode ${bootmode}
fi
...
```

So the environment changes into:

```
schema=a_b
ab_selector=b
bootname=boot
rootname=root_b
image=fitimage_b
bootmode=normal
```

Then, when U-Boot asks for the partition numbers with the `part number` command, we have that `bootpart` is still 2, but `rootpart` is now set to 4! So when we do the code:

```
...
echo Booting from mmc ...; " \
setenv bootargs '... console=${console} \
```

```
        device=/dev/mmcblk${mmcdev} root=/dev/mmcblk${mmcdev}
        p${rootpart} \
        initramfs_${bootmode} boot_schema=${schema} root_
        name=${rootname}'
bootm

...
```

the kernel command line has the following relevant settings (as already reported in the kernel messages above):

```
device=/dev/mmcblk2
root=/dev/mmcblk2p4
initramfs_normal
boot_schema=rescue
root_name=root_b
```

Note that, after a system-update, the above values will turn into

```
device=/dev/mmcblk2
```

```
root=/dev/mmcblk2p3
```

```
initramfs_normal
```

```
boot_schema=rescue
```

```
root_name=root_a
```

See the section "Doing a System-Update" below.

This time, the `init` program will do something similar as per the rescue schema, but with the following small differences:

1) This step is the same as above: the boot partition is mounted under the /boot directory, and the root filesystem encryption key is loaded.

2) The root filesystem encryption key is stored again within the kernel keyring, but with a little difference: now the variable `rootdev` points to root_b (or root_a) instead of root.

Note that we have used the same key for *root_a* and *root_b*, but we can imagine using different keys.

So, when the command is executed:

```
dmsetup create root --table \"0 $(get_blockdev_
size ${rootdev}) crypt capi:tk(cbc(aes))-plain
:36:logon:logkey: 0 ${rootdev} 0\""
```

the /dev/mapper/root is connected to the root_b (or root_a) partition instead of root (see Figure 3-2).

3) This step is the same as above: the encrypted root filesystem is mounted.

4) Then we enter again into the real root filesystem (or hang in case of errors), but before doing this, we have to do the following (extra) steps:

```
...
info "entering rootfs on $rootdev..."
move_mountpoint /dev /proc /sys /tmp
```

```
    [ -f /etc/fw_env.config ] && \
        cp --parents /etc/fw_env.config $ROOT_DIR
if [ "$schema" == a_b ] ; then
        printf "$(cat /etc/rootfs.key | sed 's/\
        (..\)/\\x\1/g')" | \
                keyctl padd logon rootfskey:fitimage @u
        cp --parents /etc/rootfs.iv $ROOT_DIR
        cp --parents /etc/caam/rootfs.key $ROOT_DIR
fi
cp --parents /etc/rootfs.sign.key $ROOT_DIR
exec switch_root -c /dev/console $ROOT_DIR ${init:
-/sbin/init}
...
```

In the section "Doing a Normal Boot" earlier in
the chapter, we replaced the code in the if clause
because, for the rescue schema, it is not executed;
however, now the situation is different, and we must
properly manage the root filesystem keys. In fact,
the root filesystem archive key (and the relative IV)
are needed to be able to decrypt an update package,
while the real root filesystem key is needed to be
able to mount the alternate root partition (i.e.,
root_a or root_b).

Note that this last step can be omitted in the case we decide to
mount both root_a and root_b within the initramfs; however, we
prefer to mount the current active root partition and then mount the
alternate one during an update only.

To securely pass the root filesystem archive encryption key to the applications in the real root filesystem we use a logon key, while the relative initial vectors (the `rootfs.iv` file) and the real root filesystem key (the `rootfs.key` file) can simply be copied in the real root filesystem due to the fact the former is not a secret and the latter is a wrapped key.

Again, the reader should note that in the case we don't use a CAAM (or equivalent) equipped CPU, we can use another logon key to do the job.

In order to show a functional example, below are reported the messages from our system during the A/B schema boot stage:

```
...
[    3.959349] Run /init as init process
init: factory_reset: subprocess 02-factory-reset.sh not
enabled! Skipped
init: resize_partitions: subprocess 05-resize-partitions.sh not
enabled! Skipped
init: system_update: subprocess 10-system-update.sh not
enabled! Skipped
[    4.079514] EXT4-fs (mmcblk2p1): recovery complete
[    4.085196] EXT4-fs (mmcblk2p1): mounted filesystem 8ce4dcd5
-5c98-4548-9155-9146831e62fd r/w with ordered data mode. Quota
mode: none.
[    4.111378] EXT4-fs (mmcblk2p1): unmounting filesystem 8ce4d
cd5-5c98-4548-9155-9146831e62fd.
422245814
669613324
```

```
init: checking rootfs on /dev/mapper/root...
e2fsck 1.47.0 (5-Feb-2023)
root: clean, 22554/256000 files, 261472/1024000 blocks
init: mounting rootfs on /dev/mapper/root...
[    5.118606] EXT4-fs (dm-0): mounted filesystem
6c744729-47cf-4b96-bd82-9b0a1f25593c r/w with ordered data
mode. Quota mode: none.
init: entering rootfs on /dev/mapper/root...
88051060
[    5.577330] systemd[1]: System time before build time,
         advancing clock.
...
[    5.667853] systemd[1]: Detected architecture arm64.

Welcome to BNDL Distro with XWayland 6.6-scarthgap (scarthgap)!
...
```

As we can see, by looking at the section "Doing a Normal Boot" earlier in the chapter, from the user perspective, the functioning is very similar to the rescue schema.

3.2.2 Doing a Factory-Reset

When we ask to do a factory-reset by setting bootmode=factory, U-Boot starts, and it detects which is the actual factory partition:

```
...
Running bootcmd [factory] on mmc2...
switch to partitions #0, OK
mmc2(part 0) is current device
Schema: A/B [selector=b]
...
```

Note also that, by default, the active partition is b. This is because, during the image generation, we have stored all factory images into the *root_a* partition (as described in the section "Rescue Schema").

Then it loads the fitimage file from it and then executes the kernel in it with the following command line:

```
...
[    0.000000] Kernel command line: console=ttymxc1,115200
device=/dev/mmcblk2 root=/dev/mmcblk2p4 rootwait rw initramfs_
factory boot_schema=a_b root_name=root_b
[    0.000000] Unknown kernel command line parameters
"initramfs_factory device=/dev/mmcblk2 boot_schema=a_b root_
name=root_b", will be passed to user space.
...
```

The parameter that specifies to do a factory-reset boot is `initramfs_factory`, and now the U-Boot metacode looks like the following:

```
...
if test ${bootmode} = normal ; then
        ...
elif test ${bootmode} = factory ; then
        setenv bootname factory
        if test ${schema} = a_b ; then
                setenv bootname root_a
                setenv rootname root_b
        fi
elif test ${bootmode} = update; then
        ...
else
        panic \"### PANIC ### Unknow bootmode ${bootmode}
```

```
fi
part number mmc ${mmcdev} $bootname bootpart; " \
part number mmc ${mmcdev} $rootname rootpart; " \
...
```

The trick is to set `bootname` pointing to `root_a`, where the factory files have been placed, and to set `rootname` pointing to `root_b`, where the initial root filesystem must be created. Then everything works as per the rescue schema! In fact, the `init` program will do something similar as per the rescue schema, but with the following small differences:

1) Initial variables now have the following settings: `schema` is set to `a_b`, while `device` and `root_name` are set, respectively, as `/dev/mmcblk2` (unchanged) and `root_b`.

2) The factory partition is still needed, so let's mount it again. However, after the factory mount, we have some supplemental steps to do:

```
...
mkdir_if_not_exist /factory
mount -o ro $factpart /factory || \
        fatal "cannot read factory
        partition"

if [ "$schema" == a_b ] ; then
        local rootapart=$(get_device_by_
        label $device root_a)
        [ -z "$rootapart" ] && \
                fatal "cannot detect
                root_a partition"
        info "mounting root_a on
        $rootapart..."
        mkdir_if_not_exist /root_a
```

```
mount -o ro $rootapart /
 root_a || \
         fatal "cannot read root_a
         partition"
factpath="/root_a"

fit_label="fitimage_b"
fi

...
```

In the rescue schema, all factory files are present within the factory partition, but now the situation is different: the root filesystem archive file and its credential are stored within the *root_a* partition, so let's mount it too.

3) Now we can go further and check the root filesystem archive's signature as done before (note that, regarding the rescue schema, now the `factpart` variable points to the `/root_a` directory instead of `/factory`).

4) The boot partition can now be created and filled as before.

5) The root filesystem is created also.

6) The partition table is rebuilt.

7) And, finally, the root directory is repopulated as per the rescue schema.

8) Now we can wipe all partitions without touching the *factory*, *boot*, and *root* partitions, because we need them to do a normal boot.

9) During the root filesystem finalization, we must do
    an extra step, which is

```
...
umount /factory
if [ "$schema" == a_b ] ; then
        umount /root_a
fi
umount /mnt
dmsetup remove root
...
```

Compared to the rescue schema, now we have to
unmount the *root_a* partition too.

10) The last step is again the notification for the
     bootloader that on the next boot we must do a
     normal boot.

In order to show a functional example, below are reported the
messages from our system during the factory-reset procedure for the
A/B schema.

The output has been broken up into several pieces to be able to
explain each step as soon as they appear in the listing.

The init process starts, and a factory-reset request has been detected:

```
...
[    4.055525] Run /init as init process
[    5.119419]  mmcblk2: p1 p2 p3 p4 p5
The operation has completed successfully.
init: factory_reset: mounting factory on /dev/mmcblk2p2...
```

```
[    5.165376] EXT4-fs (mmcblk2p2): mounted filesystem
3c828c3e-e00b-4f47-a64f-23a82ab25866 ro with ordered data mode.
Quota mode: none.
init: factory_reset: mounting root_a on /dev/mmcblk2p3...
[    5.215195] EXT4-fs (mmcblk2p3): mounted filesystem
2bb2cb4d-2f19-4e77-9619-25d3787bc83e ro with ordered data mode.
Quota mode: none.
...
```

Here both `factory` and `root_a` partitions have been mounted, so we can start building the boot partition:

```
...
Verified OK
init: factory_reset: repopulating boot on /dev/mmcblk2p1
[ext4]...
[    6.559048] EXT4-fs (mmcblk2p1): mounted filesystem
8ce4dcd5-5c98-4548-9155-9146831e62fd r/w with ordered data
mode. Quota mode: none.
init: factory_reset: generating rootfs private key...
[    8.608317] EXT4-fs (mmcblk2p1): unmounting filesystem
8ce4dcd5-5c98-4548-9155-9146831e62fd.
...
```

When finished, we rebuild the partition table for the current mass storage device:

```
...
init: factory_reset: deleting partition #3 root_a on /dev/
mmcblk2...
Warning: The kernel is still using the old partition table.
The new table will be used at the next reboot or after you
```

```
run partprobe(8) or kpartx(8)
The operation has completed successfully.
init: factory_reset: deleting partition #4 root_b on /dev/
mmcblk2...
Warning: The kernel is still using the old partition table.
The new table will be used at the next reboot or after you
run partprobe(8) or kpartx(8)
The operation has completed successfully.
init: factory_reset: deleting partition #5 data on /dev/
mmcblk2...
Warning: The kernel is still using the old partition table.
The new table will be used at the next reboot or after you
run partprobe(8) or kpartx(8)
The operation has completed successfully.
Error: Partition(s) 3 on /dev/mmcblk2 have been written, but we
have been unable to inform the kernel of the change, probably
because it/they are in use.  As a result, the old partition(s)
will remain in use.  You should reboot now before making
further changes.
```

Readers should note here that the system informs us that the partition 3 (*root_a*) is in use, and then it will remain in use. This is precisely what we want, since this partition holds all factory files we need to finish the current factory-update procedure!

```
init: factory_reset: creating partition #3 root_a
[ext4@0:+4000M]...
Warning: The kernel is still using the old partition table.
The new table will be used at the next reboot or after you
run partprobe(8) or kpartx(8)
```

```
The operation has completed successfully.
init: factory_reset: creating partition #4 root_b
[ext4@0:+4000M]...
Warning: The kernel is still using the old partition table.
The new table will be used at the next reboot or after you
run partprobe(8) or kpartx(8)
The operation has completed successfully.
init: factory_reset: creating partition #5 data [ext4@0:0]...
Warning: The kernel is still using the old partition table.
The new table will be used at the next reboot or after you
run partprobe(8) or kpartx(8)
The operation has completed successfully.
...
```

Now the encrypted root filesystem on partition *root_b* must be formatted, repopulated, and then finalized as before:

```
...
init: factory_reset: formatting root_b on /dev/mmcblk2p4 with
cipher...
221645835
35784194
[   17.652181] EXT4-fs (dm-0): mounted filesystem
6c744729-47cf-4b96-bd82-9b0a1f25593c r/w with ordered data
mode. Quota mode: none.
init: factory_reset: repopulating root_b on /dev/mapper/root
[ext4]...
init: factory_reset: resizing partition #5 data...
init: factory_reset: wiping partition data on /dev/mmcblk2p5
[ext4]...
init: factory_reset: finalizing the rootfs...
[   74.699650] EXT4-fs (mmcblk2p2): unmounting filesystem
3c828c3e-e00b-4f47-a64f-23a82ab25866.
```

```
[   74.778976] EXT4-fs (mmcblk2p3): unmounting filesystem 2bb2c
b4d-2f19-4e77-9619-25d3787bc83e.
[   77.935483] EXT4-fs (dm-0): unmounting filesystem
6c744729-47cf-4b96-bd82-9b0a1f25593c.
init: factory_reset: done!
...
```

Now the factory-update is finished, and the system can do a normal boot, as we got above for the rescue schema:

```
...
init: resize_partitions: subprocess 05-resize-partitions.sh not
enabled! Skipped
init: system_update: subprocess 10-system-update.sh not
enabled! Skipped
[   78.089405] EXT4-fs (mmcblk2p1): mounted filesystem
8ce4dcd5-5c98-454
8-9155-9146831e62fd r/w with ordered data mode. Quota
mode: none.
[   78.115532] EXT4-fs (mmcblk2p1): unmounting filesystem 8ce4d
cd5-5c98-4548-9155-9146831e62fd.
955223378
252785379
init: checking rootfs on /dev/mapper/root...
e2fsck 1.47.0 (5-Feb-2023)
root: clean, 22518/256000 files, 261329/1024000 blocks
init: mounting rootfs on /dev/mapper/root...
[   78.244544] EXT4-fs (dm-0): mounted filesystem
6c744729-47cf-4b96-bd82-9b0a1f25593c r/w with ordered data
mode. Quota mode: none.
init: entering rootfs on /dev/mapper/root...
```

```
92416251
...
[   78.790343] systemd[1]: Detected architecture arm64.

Welcome to BNDL Distro with XWayland 6.6-scarthgap (scarthgap)!
...
```

Now the system is ready to do a normal boot.

3.2.3 Doing a System-Update

Compared to the rescue schema, this time, the update procedure starts
and executes entirely in user space; the bootloader has no duties to do.

In fact, the bootloader metacode looks like the following:

```
...
if test ${bootmode} = normal ; then
        ...
elif test ${bootmode} = factory ; then
        ...
elif test ${bootmode} = update; then
        setenv bootname data;
        setenv image update/fitimage;
        if test ${schema} = a_b ; then
                panic "### PANIC ### Cannot update (A/B
                schema)!"
        fi
else
        panic "### PANIC ### Unknown bootmode ${bootmode}"
fi
...
```

In the case that bootmode is set to update and schema is a_b a system
panic is generated and the system hangs.

This is logical since the A/B schema is adopted when our system must be always running and functional, even during a system-update! In this situation we still use the `bundle-update.sh` tool, but this time we execute the code for the A/B schema. Relevant code is reported below, split into several pieces for better readability:

```
...
if [ $schema == a_b ] ; then
        root_name=$(get_cmdline_value root_name)
        if [ "$root_name" == root_a ] ; then
                root_name="root_b"
                fit_label="fitimage_b"
                ab_selector="b"
        elif [ "$root_name" == root_b ] ; then
                root_name="root_a"
                fit_label="fitimage_a"
                ab_selector="a"
        else
                fatal "cannot get alternate partition name!"
        fi
        rootdev=$(get_device_by_label $device $root_name)
        rootfstype=$(storage_info_get_fstype_by_label
        $root_name)
...
```

Firstly, we must detect the current root partition (root_a or root_b) and then derive the alternate one where the update files must be installed. Then we check the update credentials:

```
...
        blob_extract_and_link $blob $BUNDLE_ROOTFS_SIGN /tmp \
                rootfs.signature || \
```

```
                fatal "cannot get the rootfs
                signature!"
info "checking new rootfs signature..."
blob_extract $blob $BUNDLE_ROOTFS_IMG | \
        openssl dgst -verify /etc/rootfs.sign.
        key -sha256 \
                -signature /tmp/rootfs.signature || \
                        fatal "invalid rootfs
                        signature"
```

...

If everything is OK, we can proceed to install the fitimage into the boot
partition:

...

```
info "installing the $fit_label in /boot..."
blob_extract_and_rename $blob $BUNDLE_FIT_IMG /boot
$fit_label || \
        fatal "cannot install the fitimage!"
if [ $BUNDLE_KIND == "secured" ] ; then
        cat /factory/dek >> /boot/$fit_label || \
                fatal "cannot append dek file to
                fitimage"
fi
```

...

Note that we put the fitimage into /boot with a proper name, that is,
fitimage_a or fitimage_b (the name is stored in fit_label) according to
the partition we are going to update.

As explained above, the dek file is managed as optional, allowing a non-secured system to execute a system-update procedure.

Again, as per the rescue schema, at this point we should also check both fitimage and root filesystem signatures to be sure that something wrong has been provided to update the system.

Now we have to format and then remount the alternate root partition by using the root filesystem encryption key generated during the factory-reset (see above):

```
...
        info "formatting $root_name on $rootdev with cipher..."
        sh -c "keyctl new_session ; \
                keyctl padd logon logkey: @s < /etc/caam/
                rootfs.key ; \
                dmsetup --noudevsync create $root_name --table
                \"0 $(get_blockdev_size ${rootdev}) crypt
                capi:tk(cbc(aes))-plain :36:logon:logkey
: 0 $rootdev 0\""
        dmsetup mknodes $root_name
        rootdev="/dev/mapper/$root_name"
        mkfs.${rootfstype} -q -F -L root -I 256 $rootdev
        mount -t ${rootfstype} $rootdev /mnt
...
```

Doing this mount is nothing special since the encryption key is protected by the CAAM. On the other hand, for systems without a CAAM (or similar device), we must prepare this key loaded in a logon key. This will be more clear below when we see how to decrypt the root filesystem update archive.

Now a crucial step: we must install our update files into the just formatted alternate root filesystem partition, and to do so we must use the encryption key for the root filesystem TAR archive (see the section "Updating the System (System-Update)" in Chapter 2), which for the rescue schema lives only within the initramfs (file /etc/rootfs.key) generating no problems at all; but now we need this key in the root filesystem! To solve the issue, we should recall what we did in step 4 of the section "Doing a Normal Boot" under the "A/B Schema" section where we used a logon key to securely save this important key.

By using the crypto-afalg tool, we can now safely decrypt the updating root filesystem archive and repopulate the alternate root partition:

```
...

        info "repopulating $root_name on $rootdev
        [$rootfstype]..."
        keyctl link @u @s
        blob_extract $blob $BUNDLE_ROOTFS_IMG | \
                crypto-afalg decrypt aes-256-cbc \
                        -S logon,rootfskey:fitimage \
                        -V $(cat /etc/rootfs.iv) | \
                tar xJf - -C /mnt || \
                        fatal "cannot create rootfs partition"

...
```

Then the final steps: we have to fix the /etc/fstab file as done above, and then we can release all used resources:

```
...

        info "finalizing the rootfs..."
        storage_info_fix_fstab_entry $device /mnt

        umount /mnt
```

```
        dmsetup --noudevsync remove $root_name

        info "done!"
...
```

Now the update is finished, and we can prepare for booting the new code by properly selecting the ab_selector variable within the bootloader's environment:

```
...

        fw_setenv ab_selector $ab_selector || \
                fatal "cannot set the ab_selector!"
        info "A/B selector is now set to \"$ab_selector\". So,
        just reboot to run the new release!"
else
...
```

Now we can simply do a reboot or, in the case we need to move some important files from the current root partition to the new one, we can use the bundle-backup.sh command to do the job.

To show a functional example, we can do as reported below:

```
$ bundle-update.sh /data/root-image_imx8mp-icore_v0.90.bundle
bundle-update.sh: checking new rootfs signature...
Verified OK
bundle-update.sh: installing the fitimage_a in /boot...
bundle-update.sh: formatting root_a on /dev/mmcblk2p3 with
cipher...
566114035
803897591
[  630.873810] EXT4-fs (dm-1): mounted filesystem e88da94b-
c959-47d4-9cb2-11e2340cc69d r/w with ordered data mode. Quota
mode: none.
```

```
bundle-update.sh: repopulating root_a on /dev/mapper/root_a
[ext4]...
bundle-update.sh: finalizing the rootfs...
[  687.705759] EXT4-fs (dm-1): unmounting filesystem e88da94b-
c959-47d4-9cb2-11e2340cc69d.
bundle-update.sh: done!
bundle-update.sh: A/B selector is now set to "a". So, just
reboot to run the new release!
```

Now the tool works differently against the earlier section "Doing a System-Update" in this chapter; now it does all the above steps and does the system-update. Now we prefer to copy some configuration files to the newly installed system:

```
$ bundle-backup.sh copy
bundle-backup.sh: stopping service systemd-networkd.service...
Stopping 'systemd-networkd.service', but its triggering units
are still
active:
systemd-networkd.socket
bundle-backup.sh: mounting root_a on /dev/mmcblk2p3 with
cipher...
555823931
394623216
[ 2113.951425] EXT4-fs (dm-1): mounted filesystem e88da94b-
c959-47d4-9cb2-11e2340cc69d r/w with ordered data mode. Quota
mode: none.
bundle-backup.sh: copying data from files list /etc/bundle/
backup.conf in root_a...
etc/systemd/network/50-eth0.network
...
etc/ssh/ssh_host_rsa_key
```

```
etc/ssh/ssh_host_rsa_key.pub
bundle-backup.sh: done!
bundle-backup.sh: starting service systemd-networkd.service...
bundle-backup.sh: done
```

Note that this time we have used the argument copy to specify that we are not interested in creating a simple backup archive, but we wish to copy some files to the alternate directory.

Now we can do a reboot command and verify that the alternate partition is now the current one; in fact, the bootloader messages are now:

```
...
Running bootcmd [normal] on mmc2...
switch to partitions #0, OK
mmc2(part 0) is current device
Schema: A/B [selector=a]
...
```

The kernel messages are also changed:

```
...
[    0.000000] Kernel command line: console=ttymxc1,115200
device=/dev/mmcblk2 root=/dev/mmcblk2p3 rootwait rw initramfs_
normal boot_schema=a_b root_name=root_a
[    0.000000] Unknown kernel command line parameters
"initramfs_normal device=/dev/mmcblk2 boot_schema=a_b root_
name=root_a", will be passed to user space.
...
```

And the new release is now executed.

3.3 Summary

This chapter explored the practical implementation of reliable and secure Linux-based operating systems for diverse embedded and industrial devices. A central focus was placed on ensuring reliable system recovery and updates without specialized user intervention, which requires careful organization of system components on the mass storage device. We provided a deep dive into the mass storage partitioning and the boot process logic (specifically the rescue schema), which are foundational for building robust, secure, and easily maintainable embedded Linux systems.

## CHAPTER 4

Final Considerations

In previous chapters, we have seen how Secure Boot works and how we can implement a functional system under two different booting schemas. However, before closing this book, we should spend a few words on doing some practical examples about how to effectively generate encryption and signing keys and about some licensing issues we must consider when we design a secure system.

4.1 Generating Keys for Crypting and Signing

In this book, we have seen several techniques to implement a good Chain-of-Trust to be sure that the Secure Boot is correctly managed by the hardware and software. However, we never talked about how we can effectively do encryption and signature for any single image that composes the Chain-of-Trust.

Regarding the root filesystem, these operations are quite trivial; in fact, as seen in the section "Doing a Factory-Reset" in Chapter 3, for instance, a root filesystem can be encrypted or signed via OpenSSL (or any other crypting tool) in the static case, while for the runtime one, block-level encryption is the solution (see "The Block-Level Encryption" section in Chapter 1).

© Rodolfo Giometti 2026
R. Giometti, *Secure Boot Encryption with Linux,* Apress Pocket Guides,
https://doi.org/10.1007/979-8-8688-2818-8_4

On the other hand, about the bootloaders (ATF, U-Boot, etc.) and the fitimage (kernel, DTB, etc.) we never enter into details in those sections; so, now it's time to explain a bit better these aspects.

Keep in mind that each CPU vendor employs a unique approach for these steps. Therefore, the following sections maintain a general discussion. For concrete examples, however, we present two specific solutions that can be readily adapted to other platforms.

4.1.1 The Fuse-Centric Approach

This approach is based on the fact that all cryptographic secrets are held in protected FUSEs; that is, both the encryption key and the signing public key (or its hash, to save space) are securely fused into the chip.

Protected FUSEs are designed to enhance security by restricting direct access from the *normal world* (for instance, the kernel and its applications). Only the *secured world* (like ATF and OPTEE) can read these FUSEs. Consequently, any attempt by a compromised Linux OS to read the secrets stored in the FUSEs must still go through the secured world, preventing direct access to sensitive information.

When the secure boot is enabled, the ROM code is hardcoded to load the initial image (usually holding the bootloaders and the OPTEE) and verify it. As a practical example, we can consider how Secure Boot works on the STM32MP1x CPU family (see `https://wiki.st.com/stm32mpu/wiki/STM32_MPU_ROM_code_secure_boot`).

In this architecture, the public key used for signature verification is not directly stored in the FUSEs, but it is packed into the initial image, as shown in Figure 4-1.

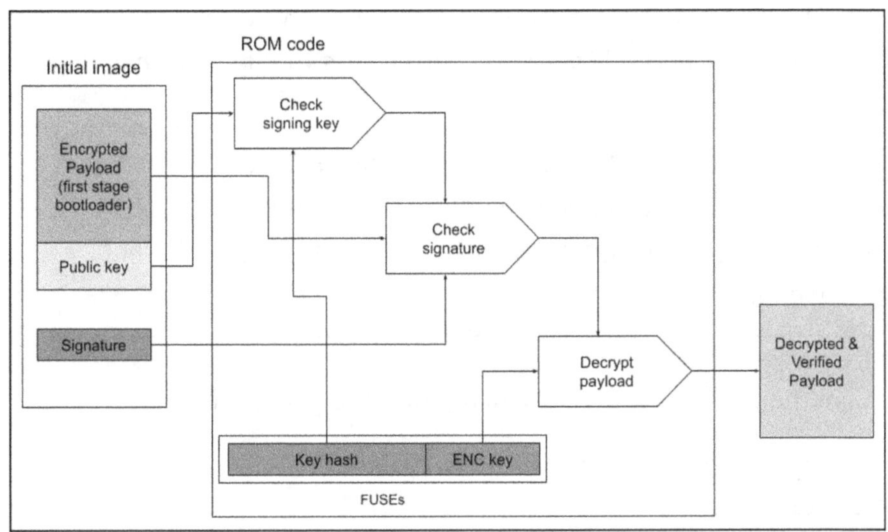

Figure 4-1. *The STM32MP1x initial image loading*

The ROM code loads this initial image and then, as a first step, checks the public key against the hash stored in the FUSEs. If the hash matches, then the key is validated, and it can be used to check the signature. If the signature is also verified, the last step is to decrypt the payload to get the code to execute to go further into the boot stage.

To create the signature key, we can use the STM32_KeyGen_CLI utility from ST, as reported below:

```
$ STM32_KeyGen_CLI -abs stm32mp13-key/ \
    -pwd azerty azerty azerty azerty azerty azerty azerty
    azerty -n 8
...
--------------------------------------------------------------
Hash of table of Hash of {algorithm + public Key} file
generated successfully.
+ Hash Hash:  stm32mp13-key/publicKeysHashHashes.bin
```

where the option argument -n is used to specify how many key pairs we wish to generate, and -pwd specifies the password for each pair.

The STM32MP1x family supports eight key pairs, and in the above example, we have used eight identical passwords set to azerty. However, on real implementation we should use eight different passwords!

For the encryption key, we can use the following command:

```
$ STM32_KeyGen_CLI -rand 16 stm32mp13-key/stm32mp_
encryption_key.bin
```

where the option argument -rand is used to generate random data (the size is specified in the next parameter) and save the result in a binary file.

At this point, within the file publicKeysHashHashes.bin is stored the public keys hash, and within the file stm32mp_encryption_key.bin is stored the encryption key. So, we can put these files in a mass storage (USB key or SD card) and then load them in the FUSEs by using the following procedure in U-Boot:

```
STM32MP> stm32key select PKHTH
STM32MP> load mmc 0:1 ${loadaddr} publicKeysHashHashes.bin
STM32MP> md.b ${loadaddr} 20
c2000000: 0b 96 b7 84 a5 56 0e 9c 4c 12 51 0f 4f 3a 47
19  .....V..L.Q.O:G.
c2000010: 76 9d 6e 0b 8b b7 0b 58 a3 48 72 5a 71 75 ef
3b  v.n....X.HrZqu.;
STM32MP> stm32key fuse ${loadaddr}
STM32MP> stm32key read
PKHTH OTP 24: 0b96b784 lock : 50000000
PKHTH OTP 25: a5560e9c lock : 50000000
```

```
PKHTH OTP 26: 4c12510f lock : 50000000
PKHTH OTP 27: 4f3a4719 lock : 50000000
PKHTH OTP 28: 769d6e0b lock : 50000000
PKHTH OTP 29: 8bb70b58 lock : 50000000
PKHTH OTP 30: a348725a lock : 50000000
PKHTH OTP 31: 7175ef3b lock : 50000000
```

In the example, we have used a microSD.

By using the `stm32key select` PKHTH command, we select the *Public Key Hash Table Hash* area in the FUSEs, and then we do the burning. On the other hand, for the encryption key, we must select the Encrypted Device Master Key area in the FUSEs and then do the burning as shown below:

```
STM32MP> stm32key select EDMK
STM32MP> load mmc 0:1 ${loadaddr} stm32mp13_encryption_key.bin
STM32MP> md.b ${loadaddr} 10
c2000000: 58 f7 76 94 23 b2 41 d0 5f ee 7d 0c 9b 2a b9
48  X.v.#.A._.}..*.H
STM32MP> stm32key fuse ${loadaddr}
STM32MP> stm32key read
EDMK OTP 92: 58f77694 lock : 40000000
EDMK OTP 93: 23b241d0 lock : 40000000
EDMK OTP 94: 5fee7d0c lock : 40000000
EDMK OTP 95: 9b2ab948 lock : 40000000
```

Now all secrets are in place, and we can go further in securing our system.

4.1.2 The Hybrid Approach

This approach is different from the previous one because, in this case, only the public key hash is stored in the FUSEs, while the encryption key is securely provided by a wrapped file stored on a mass storage. So, regarding the signature checking, nothing changes against the previous example, while for the decryption, the system first unwraps the encryption key and then starts the decryption.

This mechanism is used by the i.MX CPU family by NXP, where the wrapped file that protects the encryption key is named *DEK blob* (See Figure 4-2).

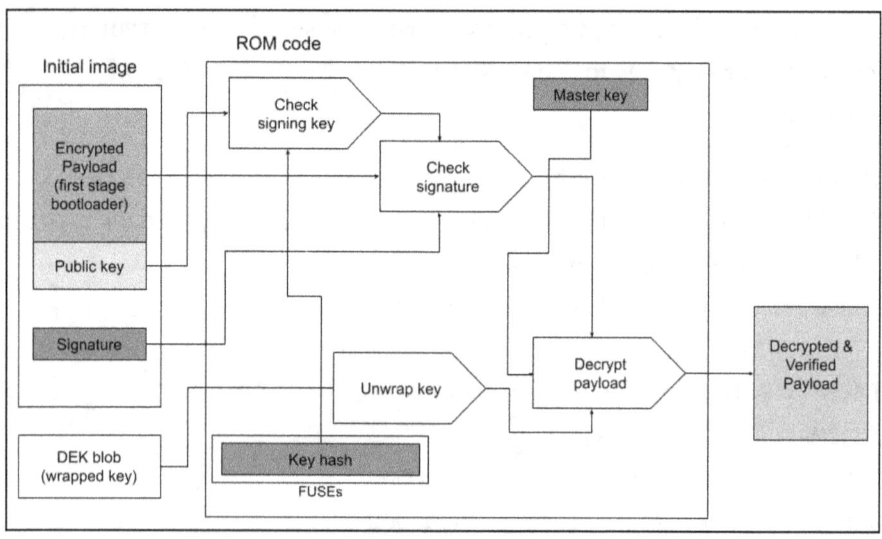

Figure 4-2. *The i.MX initial image loading*

In this situation, the ROM code must also load the DEK blob file besides the initial image to be able to properly decrypt the first-stage bootloader, while, regarding the signature checking, the procedure is similar to the above.

The key generation can be done by using a specific tool by NXP named cst (it can be downloaded at https://www.nxp.com/webapp/sps/download/license.jsp?colCode=IMX_CST_TOOL). Once downloaded and installed, we must enter into its main directory, which should look like the following:

```
$ ls
add-ons       Dockerfile.hsm   linux32
BUILD.md      docs             linux64
ca            keys             Makefile
code          LICENSE.bsd3     mingw32
crts          LICENSE.hidapi   Release_Notes.txt
Dockerfile    LICENSE.openssl  Software_Content_Register_CST.txt
```

And then create a text file named serial holding eight digits (used for the certificate serial numbers):

```
$ cd keys
$ echo 1248163E > serial
```

Then a text file called key_pass.txt, which contains two lines of a password repeated twice (used to protect the generated private keys:

```
$ echo my_password | tee -a key_pass.txt > key_pass.txt
```

Now, to generate the encryption key pairs, we must run the following:

```
$ ./ahab_pki_tree.sh
```

And complete the interactive questions (our answers are reported in bold):

```
...
Key type options (confirm targeted device supports desired
key type):
Select the key type (possible values: rsa, rsa-pss, ecc)?: ecc
```

```
Enter length for elliptic curve to be used for PKI tree:
Possible values p256, p384, p521:  p384
Enter the digest algorithm to use: sha384
Enter PKI tree duration (years): 99
Do you want the SRK certificates to have the CA flag set?
(y/n)?: n
...
```

Then we must generate the hash to be stored within the FUSEs:

```
$ cd ../crts/
$ ../linux64/bin/srktool -a -d sha256 -s sha384 \
        -t SRK_1_2_3_4_table.bin \
        -e SRK_1_2_3_4_fuse.bin -f 1 -c \
SRK1_sha384_secp384r1_v3_usr_crt.pem,SRK2_sha384_secp384r1_
v3_usr_crt.pem,SRK3_sha384_secp384r1_v3_usr_crt.pem,SRK4_
sha384_secp384r1_v3_usr_crt.pem
Number of certificates     = 4
SRK table binary filename = SRK_1_2_3_4_table.bin
SRK Fuse binary filename  = SRK_1_2_3_4_fuse.bin
SRK Fuse binary dump:
SRK HASH[0] = 0x64D18B66
SRK HASH[1] = 0x481850B5
SRK HASH[2] = 0xCE544B4D
SRK HASH[3] = 0xE81E9154
SRK HASH[4] = 0x7D36B464
SRK HASH[5] = 0xD4A0388F
SRK HASH[6] = 0x0DDF24C4
SRK HASH[7] = 0x4BA3F0AC
```

Please note that in newer versions of this tool, some algorithms may no longer be available; in that case, readers will need to choose a different algorithm that meets their needs.

The HASH vector holds the data to be written in the FUSEs via U-Boot by using the following commands:

```
iMX9> fuse prog 16 0 0x64D18B67
iMX9> fuse prog 16 1 0x481850B5
iMX9> fuse prog 16 2 0xCE544B4D
iMX9> fuse prog 16 3 0xE81E9154
iMX9> fuse prog 16 4 0x7D36B464
iMX9> fuse prog 16 5 0xD4A0388F
iMX9> fuse prog 16 6 0x0DDF24C4
iMX9> fuse prog 16 7 0x4BA3F0AC
```

Note that these commands are valid for the i.MX93 and i.MX95 only!

Regarding the encryption key, we must create it and save it into a file, then we must use U-Boot to generate the DEK blob.

Firstly, we must create the encryption key as random 256-bit data:

```
$ openssl rand 32 > dek.bin
```

Then within U-Boot we must load this data into memory and call the specific dek_blob command as shown below:

```
iMX9> load mmc 0:1 ${loadaddr} stm32mp13_encryption_key.bin
iMX9> md.b ${loadaddr} 20
81000000: 81 10 ba 8e 3c 9b f2 e6 ae 0b 4b a3 6f 72 53
66  ....<.....K.orSf
```

```
81000010: c1 57 c5 7e b7 56 1b 7e be 6e 8b 8a 11 9b 63
3f  .W.~.V.~.n....c?
iMX9> dek_blob ${loadaddr} 0x81001000 256
iMX9> md.b 0x81001000 0x58
81001000: 00 58 00 81 01 20 03 00 ec e5 62 9e 53 84 c5
c5  .X... ....b.S...
81001010: 91 7f d0 38 b1 06 7f cc 1c 6c 2c 98 9e 31 1c
66  ...8.....l,..1.f
81001020: ef e0 b0 ea 96 42 83 18 33 e1 1e 88 bf 0f 1a
41  .....B..3......A
81001030: a6 a3 1f c9 8d 5e 67 94 0b 3a e1 e3 08 80 98
b3  .....^g..:......
81001040: 8d d5 54 ea e1 64 b1 02 b1 52 b8 66 35 4d 24
8e  ..T..d...R.f5M$.
81001050: 5a dd 86 25 19 3c e4 07                      Z..%.<..
```

In the example, we have used a microSD. Also note that the DEK blob file is 88 bytes in length.

Now these data must be saved somewhere within the system as done, for instance, in the section "Rescue Schema" in Chapter 3.

Before ending this section, we must point out some important notes:

1) The final DEK blob file must be generated when the CPU is already in secure mode; otherwise, the final result will not work. In fact, by design, when the CPU is not in secure mode, the master key is a dummy key, while in secure mode, it assumes its real value.

2)   Since the encryption key is not burned into FUSEs, we can easily change it. On the other side, we must provide a secure environment for the DEK blob file generation!

4.2 Licensing Issues

The chosen implementation strategy for secure boot presents significant challenges concerning open source licenses, specifically the **GNU General Public License version 3**, also called **GPLv3** for simplicity (`https://www.gnu.org/licenses/gpl-3.0.en.html`), where it states that

> *"Installation Information" for a User Product means any methods, procedures, authorization keys, or other information required to install and execute modified versions of a covered work in that User Product from a modified version of its Corresponding Source. The information must suffice to ensure that the continued functioning of the modified object code is in no case prevented or interfered with solely because modification has been made.* [Section 6—Conveying Non-Source Forms]

Since every Secure Boot implementation only accepts manufacturer-signed binaries and does not provide a simple mechanism for the final user to register their own cryptographic keys (or install their own signed kernel), it can be considered conflictual!

Such a restrictive implementation is in potential conflict with Section 6 of the GPLv3 because it fails to provide the necessary *Installation Information* for the user to exercise their right to modify

The practice of distributing software under a copyleft license (like GPL) on a hardware product that uses security measures (such as Secure Boot) to prevent the end user from installing and running modified versions of that software on the device is called **Tivoization**. The name is due to

201

Richard Stallman (and the Free Software Foundation—FSF) regarding TiVo's use of GNU GPL-licensed software on the TiVo brand digital video recorders (DVR), which actively block modified software by design (see the specific FAQ at `https://www.gnu.org/licenses/gpl-faq.html.en#Tivoization`). Stallman believes this practice denies users some of the freedom that the GNU GPL was designed to protect. So, the FSF refers to tivoized hardware as *proprietary tyrants*.

In this scenario, embedded developers should carefully check the software they use within their system or provide a mechanism to respect the GPLv3!

Currently, fundamental components like U-Boot, TFA, OP-TEE, and Linux are primarily licensed under GPLv2. Trusted Firmware and OP-TEE (for instance) are licensed under BSD or MIT, which do not impose copyleft requirements and, consequently, do not conflict with a restrictive Secure Boot implementation. This is essential since we can use them within our secured systems.

On the other hand, there are several user space applications released under the GPLv3 or, in general, under more restrictive licenses. In this scenario, we have two major choices:

1) We can decide not to use such applications at all (or rewrite them).

2) We must provide a way to be GPLv3 compliant by allowing the end user to **modify the software and re-run it on the hardware**.

This last step can be easily implemented by replacing our secured bootloader with another one that allows loading a plain text kernel, which in turn loads a plain text root filesystem. Crucially, if the secured system includes a proprietary application, this plain text root filesystem provided to the user must only contain the GPLv3 software components and must exclude the proprietary application. This separation ensures the final users will be able to modify and re-run the GPLv3 software provided in the secured system, fulfilling the requirements of Section 6 of the GPLv3 without exposing the proprietary code.

In Figure 4-3, both the secured and modified bootloaders are loaded under the Chain-of-Trust, but just in the left path the Chain-of-Trust continues. On the right one, the chain stops, allowing the end user to load whatever is within the root filesystem. On the other hand, in the left path, the proprietary code is protected by the Chain-of-trust, while in the right one, there is nothing to protect.

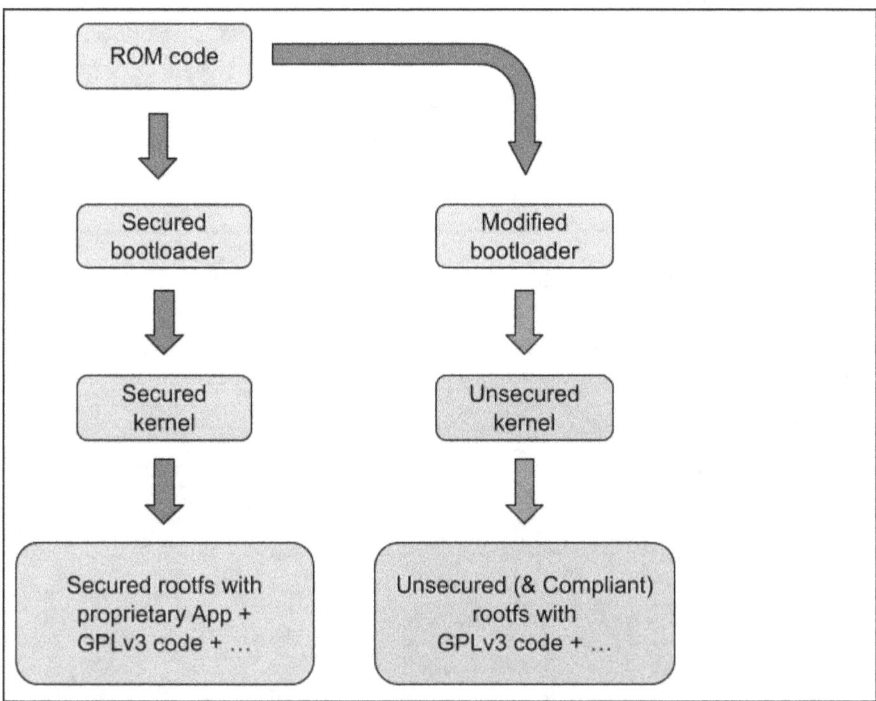

Figure 4-3. *Secured system to GPLv3 compliant system*

4.3 Summary

In this chapter, we've seen some simple examples of how to generate keys to encrypt and sign bootloaders (and fitimages) for two specific types of CPUs (although these examples aren't generic, they provide an idea of what to do to protect our systems).

We then introduced some aspects of how to keep our system compliant with GPLv3 requirements to avoid tedious (and expensive) legal battles.

At this point, it should be clearer what Secure Boot is and the steps to follow to get a working system.

Enjoy!

APPENDIX A

Notes on Tamper Detection

In high-security environments, the integrity of a system extends beyond the digital realm. In fact, a successful physical intrusion, such as opening a chassis and inserting a malicious hardware component or removing a benevolent one, allows an attacker to bypass many traditional software-based controls.

Let's think about Intelligent Electronic Devices (IED), Remote Terminal Units (RTUs), or Distributed Control Systems (DCS) for critical infrastructure (such as power grids, gas networks, and oil infrastructures), life-upport and healthcare medical devices, and fiscal measurement systems (e.g., smart meters), where hardware tampering could lead to catastrophic failures or large-scale fraud.

That's why physical tamper detection mechanisms are essential for identifying these unauthorized access attempts to the system's housing or components.

Most modern CPUs offer various mechanisms for tampering detection, which are capable of signaling the CPU if the system has been compromised and, in that case, halting the system or doing other security actions.

© Rodolfo Giometti 2026
R. Giometti, *Secure Boot Encryption with Linux*, Apress Pocket Guides,
https://doi.org/10.1007/979-8-8688-2818-8

Physical detection can be divided into two categories: **external tamper** (on the chassis/board) and **internal tamper** (on the chip itself).

The former mechanism is specifically designed to detect the opening of the chassis or the tampering of board components, and usually the processor has dedicated input pins (often called *tamper pins*) to detect these attempts.

These tamper pins are connected to a physical sensor installed on the system's enclosure, such as a simple switch that opens or closes when the chassis is opened (the most common method). Or conductive thin traces printed on the PCB or inside the chassis where their breakage or interruption, caused by an attempt to drill or force entry, triggers the alarm

Additionally, motion sensors or location-based triggers are often used in localized meters and controllers to detect unauthorized movement or physical dislocation of the device (this is because an attacker might choose not to tamper with the casing on-site, but instead detach the entire unit for analysis in a laboratory environment). In the critical infrastructure sector (energy, gas, water), devices such as smart meters are often installed in remote or publicly accessible locations, etc.

To control the status of these sensors, the CPU may use a **passive tamper detection**; that is, it monitors a fixed voltage level (and if the state changes, e.g., the switch opens, an alarm is activated). Alternatively, the CPU outputs a time-varying signal (typically a random or rapidly switching signal) on an output pin and expects to receive the same signal in real time on an input pin, which are connected in a pair by a wire or trace across the chassis. This latter detection mechanism is called **active tamper detection**. Of course, this method is more sophisticated and then secure.

On the other hand, the internal tampering detection is a set of mechanisms that are usually not linked to the chassis but monitor the CPU's immediate operating environment. For example, constant monitoring of the power supply voltage levels (a sudden drop or spike in voltage can indicate a physical attack attempt or an attempt to force a chip reset) or temperature monitoring (too high or too low temperature can indicate an attack, e.g., freezing the chip to alter memory or overheating) or by monitoring the system clock frequency (clock tampering is an attack technique to disrupt or slow down the processor).

Once a tampering access has been detected, the most critical feature of a good tampering system is its response, which must be immediate and destructive to sensitive data. Firstly, an alarm flag in a dedicated register (*sentinel*) is set; then the most common and crucial reaction is the *zeroization* (or erasure) of the volatile memory containing sensitive data (usually the master cryptographic keys to render all encrypted data unusable). Moreover, the CPU can also force a system reset or put itself into a locked state until the tampering is resolved (see below about tampering recovery

To implement a good tampering detection system, modern CPUs are usually split into two main regions:

1)   A normal region that is normally powered

2)   A special region that is battery-backed

Note that when we mention the battery-backed part, we are not referring to a whole battery-backed system but just a single region of the CPU typically named as **Battery-Backed Secure Module** (or **Secure Non-Volatile Module** or Storage). Typically, this region has a battery that is not the main system battery (when present), and it is well embedded in the main board. We can name it as *tampering battery*, and its only target is to keep the secure module powered on even when the main power is not present. This is crucial if we need to detect tampering accesses under all circumstances; in fact, by properly setting up the *sentinel* register, we can detect whether this battery has been removed or not (see below about how this register can be used).

The battery-backed region is also not directly accessible by the normal world (which is unprivileged), but it must be accessed through a privileged supervisor. For example, on ARM-based systems, the supervisor can be either the ATF or OP-TEE according to the specific boot stage.

In Figure A-1 is reported a generic example of a tamper detection system.

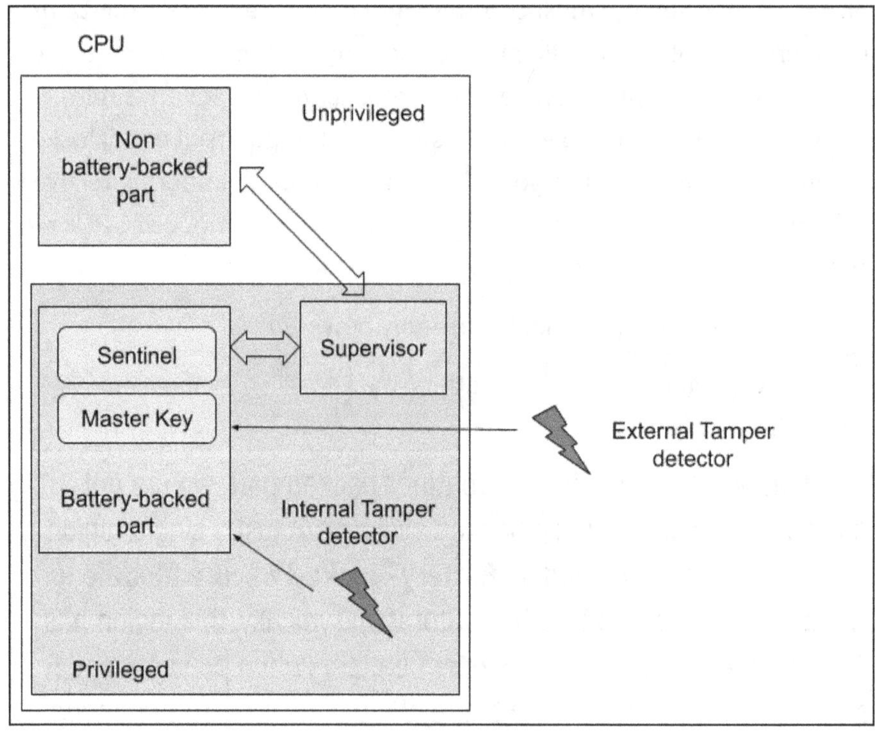

Figure A-1. *Tamper detection system*

Note that even if both the *sentinel* and *master key* registers default to 0, in the case of tampering battery faults, we cannot use the latter in place of the former. In most cases, the master key register is a write-only register.

A.1 Tampering During the Boot

The tampering detection can be used to verify the Chain-of-Trust integrity during the boot, so it has an important role within the Secure Boot process (but it can be used also when the system is up and running—see below). In this scenario, the CPU running in supervisor mode can use the following code to manage the tamper detection:

```
...
/* Tampering recovery section */
if (is_tampering_init_forced() ||
    defined(CONFIG_TAMPERING_INIT_FORCED)) {
        setup_tampering_battery_status();
        if (ret)
                hang("cannot setup battery!");
#if defined(CONFIG_TAMPERING_INIT_FORCED)
        hang("tampering detection initialized. Reset
        the board");
#endif
        ret = unforce_tampering_init();
        if (ret)
                hang("cannot unforce tampering init!");
    }
```

```
/* Tampering enable section */
ret = enable_tamper_detection();
if (ret)
        hang("cannot enable tamper detection!");

if (!is_tampering_battery_ok())
        hang("Tampering battery fault! Restart the
        system");

/* OK, let's do a normal boot! */
...
```

The first section of the above code (i.e., the *tampering recovery section*) is used to initialize or recover the system. The second one (the *tampering enable section*) is used to actually enable the tampering detection within the CPU (by using the enable_tamper_detection() function) and then to check the tampering battery status by checking the sentinel register; in this scenario, the is_tampering_battery_ok() function can be implemented as reported below:

```
static bool is_tampering_battery_ok(void)
{
        uint8_t val = read_register(SNVM_SENTINEL_REG);

        return val == SENTINEL_REGISTER_VALUE;
}
```

During the tampering recovery section (or during the initialization), the sentinel is programmed as follows:

```
static int setup_tampering_battery_status(void)
{
        return write_register(SNVM_SENTINEL_REG,
                            SENTINEL_REGISTER_VALUE);
}
```

Since the sentinel register is battery-backed, it retains the value SENTI-NEL_REGISTER_VALUE even if the main power is removed, and the system must be considered tampered in the case it holds a different value (or the default reset value).

It should be clear now what the initialization section is needed for; it must execute the setup_tampering_battery_status(). However, this operation must be done under special circumstances only:

- During the factory production or

- During a tampering recovery

In both cases, this operation must be done by specialized and authorized personnel.

During the factory production, we can force the loading of a special version of the bootloader that has the CONFIG_TAMPERING_INIT_FORCED define enabled. In this case, the bootloader starts and automatically calls setup_tampering_battery_status() before doing a hang.

On the other hand, if we wish to implement a tampering recovery procedure, we can define the is_tampering_init_forced() function in such a way that it returns *true* if the recovery must start. Then, once the sentinel register has been properly programmed, we can close the recovery procedure by using the unforce_tampering_init() function.

There are several ways to implement these two functions; however, the simplest (and most unsecure) way to do so is by using a GPIO line (eventually connected to a switch on the PCB). In this scenario, the two functions look like the following:

```
static bool is_tampering_init_forced(void)
{
        return read_gpio(FORCE_TAMPERING_INIT);
}
```

```c
static int setup_tampering_battery_status(void)
{
        hang("Release the FORCE_TAMPERING and reboot");
        return 0;
}
```

During normal functioning, the FORCE_TAMPERING_INIT is read as 0, and the initialization section is disabled, while during a tamper recovery or initialization, it reads as 1, and the setup_tampering_battery_status() function is called before doing a hang to force the GPIO release.

A more sophisticated (and secure) way to force a tampering initialization can be, for example, by reading an EEPROM that can be programmed via a dedicated (and external hardware); in this scenario, the above functions may look like the following:

```c
static bool is_tampering_init_forced(void)
{
        uint8_t val;
        int ret;

        ret = read_eeprom(FORCE_TAMPERING, &val);
        if (ret)
                return ret;

        return val;
}

static int setup_tampering_battery_status(void)
{
        return write_eeprom(FORCE_TAMPERING, 0);
}
```

There isn't a fixed rule; it depends on the security level we wish for our system. For example, an extreme solution should be to disable any recovery action by defining the above functions as shown below:

```
static bool is_tampering_init_forced(void)
{
        return false;
}

static int setup_tampering_battery_status(void)
{
        return -EINVAL;
}
```

In this situation, the only possible action is the initialization by using a dedicated bootloader with the `CONFIG_TAMPERING_INIT_FORCED` define enabled. This bootloader simply starts and executes the following code:

```
setup_tampering_battery_status();
hang("tampering detection initialized. Reset the
board");
```

Note that whoever has this special software can do a tampering recovery! So, a more secure version can use an authentication protocol over the serial line (or other communication mechanism) to decide whether the software holder is a privileged user or not before proceeding with the recovery (e.g., by using a Challenge-Response Authentication protocol).

However, these enhancements are really system-dependent, and they are not covered in this book.

A.2 Tampering During System Running

When the system is up and running, the Secure Boot duties are finished; however, for the sake of completeness, we will show how the tampering detection may work.

If a tampering event is detected, the supervisor may force a reboot (in this case we refer to the previous section), or it can send to the user space a notice (usually via the sysfs interface or a char device). In this latter case, we can use a system daemon that monitors the tampering events and then does a proper action, such as stopping the main program or deleting some files, etc.

For example, the system below exports some useful information about its CPU's status within the sysfs interface:

```
$ ls /sys/devices/soc0
family    power     secured        soc_id     tampered
machine   revision  serial_number  subsystem  uevent
$ cat /sys/devices/soc0/family
Freescale i.MX
$ cat /sys/devices/soc0/soc_id
i.MX8MQ
$ cat /sys/devices/soc0/machine
NXP imx8mq-var-dart SD+LVDS
$ cat /sys/devices/soc0/serial_number
160C89D6D8F804A2
```

Via this interface we can easily know whether the machine is in secure mode or not:

```
$ cat /sys/devices/soc0/secured
yes
```

And, by using the same interface, a user space application can detect whether the machine has been tampered with or not:

```
$ cat /sys/devices/soc0/tampered
no
```

So, by periodically monitoring this file, we can take a proper recovery action (such as doing a reboot that will cause a system hang).

Securing Secrets Across Booting Stages

In "The Chain-of-Trust" section in Chapter 2, we saw how the Chain-of-Trust works, that is, how each stage is responsible for verifying the next one before executing it. In normal functioning, all stages should be unrelated to each other. That is, what a single stage does during its execution should not depend on the previous one to ensure the chain is not broken, for example, by exchanging critical information between each stage. However, achieving this mode of operation is really challenging, especially between the bootloader and the kernel stage or between the kernel and the following initial user space stage (the initramfs).

In fact, it is really common that the bootloader passes some settings to the kernel or, through the kernel, to the user-space applications; practical examples of what we are saying are just the real implementations we have reported in the previous chapters of this book, where we have presented the Rescue and A/B schemas (see sections "Rescue Schema" and "A/B Schema" in Chapter 3). In our example, the bootloader is responsible for informing the kernel which is the current booting schema and if the kernel must execute a factory reset or a system update!

© Rodolfo Giometti 2026

R. Giometti, *Secure Boot Encryption with Linux*, Apress Pocket Guides,
https://doi.org/10.1007/979-8-8688-2818-8

For a security expert developer, this data exchange can be considered a security risk that can compromise the Chain-of-Trust. In fact, U-Boot holds its environment in some non-volatile storage devices, for instance, a block of the eMMC, a partition of a flash device, or within EEPROM, etc. Usually, the environment is not encrypted nor signed, so an attacker can alter it to gain access to the initramfs and then execute evil code or read secrets!

Readers should note that although this is not an easy task (because the attacker must gain root access through a corrupted network application or by physical access to the serial console or to the whole system in general), it's theoretically possible. So, we must consider this possibility and try to find effective fixes.

For example, if we suppose that the attacker has gained root access via the network, they can read the U-Boot's environment by using the fw_printenv command, as shown below:

```
$ fw_printenv
ab_selector=b
arch=arm
baudrate=115200
...
bootmode=normal
bootname=boot
bootpart=1
...
mmcboot=echo Booting from mmc ...; run mmcargs; setenv kernelargs
${kernelargs} initramfs_${bootmode} boot_schema=${schema} root_
name=${rootname}; run optargs; bootm ${loadaddr}#conf-${board_
sof}; echo ERROR: Cannot boot from fitimage;
mmcdev=2
```

```
optargs=setenv bootargs ${bootargs} ${kernelargs};
prepare_mcore=setenv mcore_clk clk-imx8mp.mcore_booted;
rootname=root
rootpart=2
...
```

In the above output, we can recognize some parameters to manage the A/B booting schema and how the final `bootargs` content is set. The bootargs variable contains parameters used by the kernel during boot, so the attacker can inject this setting to force the kernel to stop the `init` execution at the next boot and offer a prompt:

```
$ fw_setenv kernelargs 'rdinit=/bin/sh'
```

Each Linux user/developer should know that by default the kernel, at the end of the boot process, tries to execute the first user-space process (PID 1), which is usually stored within the `/sbin/init` file in the root filesystem. In the Linux kernel command line, we can alter this behavior by using both the `init=` and `rdinit=` option arguments, which are used to specify which program the kernel should run as the init process. The fundamental difference between these two options lies in which filesystem the kernel looks in to find that program. The former parameter tells the kernel which binary to execute from the real root filesystem (the one specified by `root=`). If not specified, the kernel traditionally tries `/sbin/init`, `/etc/init`, `/bin/init`, and finally `/bin/sh`.

We can see this behavior in the file `init/main.c` of the Linux sources:

```
static int __ref kernel_init(void *unused)
{
...
        if (ramdisk_execute_command) {
                ret = run_init_process(ramdisk_
                execute_command);
                if (!ret)
                        return 0;
                pr_err("Failed to execute %s (error
                %d)\n", ramdisk_execute_command, ret);
        }
        /*
         * We try each of these until one succeeds.
         *
         * The Bourne shell can be used instead of
           init if we are
         * trying to recover a really broken
           machine.
         */
        if (execute_command) {
                ret = run_init_process(execute_
                command);
                if (!ret)
                        return 0;
                panic("Requested init %s failed
                (error %d).", execute_command, ret);
        }
```

```
if (CONFIG_DEFAULT_INIT[0] != '\0') {
        ret = run_init_process(CONFIG_
        DEFAULT_INIT);
        if (ret)
                pr_err("Default init %s
                failed (error %d)\n",
                        CONFIG_DEFAULT_
                        INIT, ret);
        else
                return 0;
}

if (!try_to_run_init_process("/sbin/init") ||
    !try_to_run_init_process("/etc/init") ||
    !try_to_run_init_process("/bin/init") ||
    !try_to_run_init_process("/bin/sh"))
        return 0;

panic("No working init found. Try passing
init= option to kernel." "See Linux
Documentation/admin-guide/init.rst for
guidance.");
}
```

The latter parameter (`rdinit`) tells the kernel which binary to execute from the initramfs (or *initrd*—the name means RAM Disk Init). If we don't specify this, the kernel defaults to looking for /init in the initramfs. In fact, in the above code, we can see that the kernel tries to execute whatever is in `ramdisk_execute_command`, which is set at the beginning of the file as

```
static char *ramdisk_execute_command = "/init";
```

Now, on the next boot, we get on the system's serial console:

```
$ reboot
$               Stopping Session c1 of User root...
[  OK  ] Stopped target Graphical Interface.
...
[    3.717206] Freeing unused kernel memory: 43520K
[    3.721970] Run /bin/sh as init process
```

Readers should note that to work, the above trick is subject to two conditions:

1) The attacker must know exactly the correct value
   for `rdinit=`, otherwise the system will hang
   during the next reboot.

2) In the case we are using BusyBox (`https://`
   `busybox.net/`) to create our `initramfs`
   and especially to implement the `/bin/sh` shell
   process, we are safe. In fact, BusyBox is designed
   to be a compact, all-in-one utility, but when
   started with PID 1 by using `rdinit=/bin/sh`, it
   expects specific behavior from the `init` system. It
   attempts to act like a real `init`, or, if it's a shell, it
   attempts to run an initialization script.

   In particular, the second condition actually acts as
   a security measure, and when used, the attacker
   will get an error as reported below:

```
...
[    3.649832] Run /bin/sh as init process
[    3.656073] Kernel panic - not syncing: Attempted
to kill init! exitcode=0x00000200
/bin/sh: can't open 'initramfs_normal': No such file
or directory
[    1.199403] Kernel panic - not syncing: Attempted
to kill init! exitcode=0x00000200

...
```

In the next sections, we are going to propose some solutions to address these problems (especially when the rdinit=/bin/sh trick works).

B.1 Fixing the Kernel Command line

Now, let's suppose we can replace the execution of the init with a shell; we used a wrapper script named sh.sh as reported below:

```
#!/bin/sh

/bin/sh
```

In this scenario, the attacker will use the rdinit=/sh.sh option argument as shown above, and they can easily steal the static root filesystem encryption key by simply doing the following command when the prompt is ready:

```
[    3.155364] Run /sh.sh as init process
/bin/sh: can't access tty; job control turned off
~ # ls /etc/
```

```
...
rootfs.iv
rootfs.key
rootfs.sign.key
...
# cat /etc/rootfs.key
24ccd69079643e8335e2d8dbbf81cb54ad365b798c53993b3fc7fb73d8574209
```

Note that if the `/etc/rootfs.key` file is a binary file, the attacker can read it simply by executing the following command:

```
$ while IFS= read -r -n 1 char ; do \
          printf "%02x" "'$char" ; \
   done < /etc/rootfs.key
24ccd69079643e8335e2d8dbbf81cb54ad365b798c53993b3fc7f
b73d8574209
```

The first and easiest solution to address the above issue (when we can't use BusyBox) is to completely disable the `rdinit=` kernel option argument. This feature is managed in the file `init/main.c` of the kernel sources, as shown below:

```c
static int __init rdinit_setup(char *str)
{
        unsigned int i;

        ramdisk_execute_command = str;
        /* See "auto" comment in init_setup */
        for (i = 1; i < MAX_INIT_ARGS; i++)
                argv_init[i] = NULL;
```

```
        return 1;
}
__setup("rdinit=", rdinit_setup);
```

We can simply remove this code or fix it as reported below:

```
static int __init rdinit_setup(char *str)
{
        pr_warn("rdinit= option argument disabled!\n");

        return 1;
}
__setup("rdinit=", rdinit_setup);
```

Of course, the same fix can also be done for the `init=` kernel option
argument if needed.

Once the kernel is recompiled and installed, the attacker should get
something as shown below:

```
...
[    0.000000] Kernel command line: console=ttymxc1,115200
device=/dev/mmcblk2 root=/dev/mmcblk2p4 rootwait rw rdinit=/
bin/sh initramfs_normal boot_schema=a_b root_name=root_b
[    0.000000] rdinit= option argument disabled!
[    0.000000] Unknown kernel command line parameters
"initramfs_normal device=/dev/mmcblk2 boot_schema=a_b root_
name=root_b", will be passed to user space.
...
```

And the boot will continue as usual:

```
...
[    3.120893] Freeing unused kernel memory: 43520K
[    3.125603] Run /init as init process
init: factory_reset: subprocess 02-factory-reset.sh not
enabled! Skipped
init: resize_partitions: subprocess 05-resize-partitions.sh not
enabled! Skipped
init: system_update: subprocess 10-system-update.sh not
enabled! Skipped
...
```

B.2 Embedding Secrets in the Kernel

Even if all the above solutions can be used, we still have doubts about the possibility that an attacker may read our secrets from the initramfs. In the case such secrets are encryption keys, we can move such information within the kernel and protect them with the kernel keyring, as seen in "The Linux Key-Management Facility" section in Chapter 1.

For example, we can remove the static root filesystem encryption key from the file /etc/rootfs.key and put it directly within the kernel by using a kernel module.

Readers should note that using a kernel module not statically linked within the kernel is a big security hole! In fact, the embedded secret can be easily extracted from the .ko file (see below in this section).

This scenario is used as an example of how we can embed a key within the kernel code; real applications should avoid using modules at all!

Please also note that the solution presented here is intended solely as an educational example. In industrial-grade and security-critical applications, encryption keys should never be encoded directly in the source code (unless this has been carefully considered by the developers).

The code of the kernel module is quite long (and can be retrieved at `https://github.com/giometti/key-injector`), so in this book we are going to split it into several logical pieces.

The first piece is the main definition part:

```c
#define pr_fmt(fmt) "%s:%s: " fmt, KBUILD_MODNAME, __func__
#include <linux/init.h>
#include <linux/module.h>
#include <linux/kernel.h>
#include <linux/key.h>
#include <linux/key-type.h>
#include <linux/err.h>

static const unsigned char key_payload[] = {
        0x24, 0xcc, 0xd6, 0x90, 0x79, 0x64, 0x3e, 0x83,
        0x35, 0xe2, 0xd8, 0xdb, 0xbf, 0x81, 0xcb, 0x54,
        0xad, 0x36, 0x5b, 0x79, 0x8c, 0x53, 0x99, 0x3b,
        0x3f, 0xc7, 0xfb, 0x73, 0xd8, 0x57, 0x42, 0x09
};
static const size_t key_len = sizeof(key_payload);

static struct key *keyring, *key;
static const char *keyring_description = "keyring-injector",
                  *key_description = "rootfskey:fitimage";

...
```

Even if the Linux kernel programming is not covered in this book, readers knowing C programming should easily follow what we are going to explain in this section.

Within the key_payload array, we have placed the encryption key we wish to embed in the kernel, while keyring_description and key_description are used to hold, respectively, the keyring and the key names used to address our new kernel key and its keyring.

Then the main function, the key_injector_init(), which is used to inject the key_payload data into the keyring:

```c
static int __init key_injector_init(void)
{
        key_ref_t key_ref;
        int ret;

        pr_info("allocate keyring %s\n", keyring_description);
        keyring = keyring_alloc(keyring_description,
                        GLOBAL_ROOT_UID, GLOBAL_ROOT_GID,
                        current_cred(),
                        (KEY_POS_ALL & ~KEY_POS_SETATTR) | \
                                        KEY_USR_ALL | KEY_
                                        USR_LINK,
                        KEY_ALLOC_NOT_IN_QUOTA, NULL, NULL);
        if (IS_ERR(keyring)) {
                ret = PTR_ERR(keyring);
                pr_err("error allocating keyring\n");
                goto error_keyring_alloc;
        }
        pr_info("keyring %s allocated with serial #%d\n",
                        keyring_description, keyring->serial);
```

```c
        pr_info("insert logon key %s (%zu bytes)\n",
                        key_description, key_len);
        key_ref = key_create_or_update(make_key_ref(keyring,
        true), "logon", key_description,
                        (const char *) key_payload, key_len,
                        (KEY_POS_ALL & ~KEY_POS_SETATTR) | KEY_
                        USR_ALL, KEY_ALLOC_NOT_IN_QUOTA);
        if (IS_ERR(key_ref)) {
                pr_err("error inserting key\n");
                ret = PTR_ERR(key_ref);
                goto error_key_create;
        }

        ret = key_link(keyring, key_ref_to_ptr(key_ref));
        if (ret < 0) {
                pr_err("can't link key to keyring\n");
                goto error_key_link;
        }

        key = key_ref_to_ptr(key_ref);
        pr_info("logon key %s inserted with serial #%d\n",
                        key_description, key->serial);

        return 0;

error_key_link:
        key_put(key);
error_key_create:
        key_put(keyring);

error_keyring_alloc:
        return ret;
}
```

First, the function allocates the keyring where to place the key by using the function `keyring_alloc()`:

- The `keyring_description` variable is the name for the new keyring.

- The defines `GLOBAL_ROOT_UID`, `GLOBAL_ROOT_GID` set the ownership of the keyring to the root user (with UID 0 and GID 0).

- The function `current_cred()` provides the security context of the process/thread currently executing this code. The kernel uses this context to verify that the caller has the necessary permissions (e.g., capability `CAP_SYS_ADMIN`) to create a root-owned keyring.

- The permissions settings meaning is

  - `KEY_POS_ALL & ~KEY_POS_SETATTR`: Grants all kernel permissions except the permission to change the key's attributes (owner, group, or permissions)

  - `KEY_USR_ALL`: Grants all user permissions (read, write, search, link) to the keyring's owner

  - `KEY_USR_LINK`: Explicitly grants the link permission to the keyring's owner, allowing other keys to be attached to this keyring (needed to be able to execute the `keyctl link` subcommand on the keyring—see below)

  - `KEY_ALLOC_NOT_IN_QUOTA`: Allocates the keyring without counting it against the user's key quota.

If everything works well (a.k.a., no errors arise), the function uses `key_create_or_update()` to create the key and insert it into the just created keyring:

- The function `make_key_ref(keyring, true)` provides a key reference pointing to the newly created keyring as the context for creation/search.

- The `logon` string specifies the type of key being created (see "The Logon Key" section in Chapter 1).

- The `key_description` is the name of the key.

- The `key_payload` and `key_len` define the actual secret data (payload) and its length.

Again, if everything works well, the function will return success, and the key is successfully injected!

Before returning, however, the function calls `key_link()` to link the newly created key to a keyring. In fact, a key can exist in the kernel globally, but it must be linked to a keyring to be discoverable by other processes that have access to that keyring.

Then the module continues by defining the `key_injector_exit()` function, which is used when the module is unloaded:

```c
static void __exit key_injector_exit(void)
{
        if (keyring && key) {
                key_invalidate(key);
                key_unlink(keyring, key);
                key_put(key);
                pr_info("key %s (#%d) removed\n",
                                key_description, key->serial);
        }
```

```
    if (keyring) {
            key_put(keyring);
            pr_info("keyring %s (#%d) removed\n",
                            keyring_description, keyring-
                            >serial);
    }

    pr_info("module unloaded\n");
}
```

It is useless in a real example since, as explained above, this code should be statically linked within an encrypted kernel, so this function is actually never called.

Then the last (but not least) part is the module definition:

```
module_init(key_injector_init);
module_exit(key_injector_exit);

MODULE_LICENSE("GPL");
MODULE_AUTHOR("Rodolfo Giometti <giometti@enneenne.com>");
MODULE_DESCRIPTION("Inject a logon key into the kernel
keyring");
```

This is the classic way to define a kernel module, where we must inform the compiler which are the init and exit functions for the module.

As already stated, this book will not cover kernel programming nor kernel module compilation. Readers are encouraged to retrieve from the Internet how to compile and install this module on their systems.

Once the kernel starts, the key can now be accessed as usual via the keyctl tool and used by using our crypto-afalg tool as explained in "The

Linux Key-Management Facility" section in Chapter 1. To locate the key, we can use the following commands:

```
$ grep keyring-injector /proc/keys
18cfeb61 I------      1 perm 1f3f0000      0      0 keyring
keyring-injector: 1
$ keyctl show 0x18cfeb61
Keyring
 416279393 --alswrv      0      0  keyring: keyring-injector
 710245733 --alswrv      0      0  \_ logon: rootfskey:fitimage
```

The kernel module can be loaded in several ways; however, we have used the following one:

```
$ insmod /usr/lib/modules/$(uname -r)/updates/key_injector.ko
```

Once loaded, the kernel should show something as reported below:

```
[  191.415250] key_injector: loading out-of-tree module
taints kernel.
[  191.421833] key_injector:key_injector_init: allocate
keyring keyring-injector
```

```
[  191.429099] key_injector:key_injector_init: keyring
keyring-injector allocated with serial #416279393
```

```
[  191.438380] key_injector:key_injector_init: insert logon
key rootfske y:fitimage (32 bytes)
```

```
[  191.438421] key_injector:key_injector_init: logon key
rootfskey:fitim age inserted with serial #710245733
```

To prove that this injected key is the same as the one we used for the A/B schema in the section "A/B Schema" in Chapter 3, we can start by noting that in the user keyring we have the following:

```
$ keyctl show @u
Keyring
 456807198 --alswrv        0 65534  keyring: _uid.0
 403996962 --alsw-v        0     0   \_ logon: rootfskey:fitimage
```

So, we can get access to both keys by linking both the user keyring and the keyring-injector keyring to the session keyring as shown below:

```
$ keyctl link 0x18cfeb61 @s
$ keyctl link @u @s
$ keyctl show
Session Keyring
 685038700 --alswrv        0     0 keyring: _ses
 857531075 ----s-rv        0     0  \_ user: invocation_id
 456807198 --alswrv        0 65534  \_ keyring: _uid.0
 403996962 --alsw-v        0     0   |  \_ logon:
rootfskey:fitimage
 416279393 --alswrv        0     0   \_ keyring: keyring-injector
 710245733 --alswrv        0     0       \_ logon:
rootfskey:fitimage
```

In this scenario, the better way to correctly address each key is by using its serial number, so we can use the next command to encrypt a message with a key and then decrypt it with the other key:

```
$ echo 'Very secret message' | \
        crypto-afalg encrypt aes-256-cbc -S 403996962 \
            -V $(cat /etc/rootfs.iv) | \
```

```
crypto-afalg decrypt aes-256-cbc -S 710245733 \
         -V $(cat /etc/rootfs.iv)
Very secret message
```

Great! It's now shown that the two keys have the same payload.

In this scenario, the init program can avoid moving the /etc/rootfs.key content from the file to the kernel's key, as shown in the section "Doing a Normal Boot" in Chapter 3, and use the injected key directly.

Before ending this section, let's see how an attacker can find out the encryption key if they have access to the .ko file. By using a cross-toolchain, we can get the list of symbols from the kernel object file:

```
$ aarch64-linux-gnu-nm key_injector.ko
0000000000000000 T cleanup_module
0000000000000000 r __func__.0
0000000000000038 r __func__.1
0000000000000000 T init_module
0000000000000008 b key
                 U key_create_or_update
0000000000000000 t key_injector_exit
0000000000000000 t key_injector_init
                 U key_invalidate
                 U key_link
0000000000000018 r key_payload
                 U key_put
...
```

The key_payload symbol is marked with a lowercase r in the above output. This means that key_payload is a variable residing in the .rodata (Read-Only Data) section of the kernel module. The .rodata section contains read-only constant data that has been initialized in the source code.

So, to read its content, we must use `objdump` specifying the variable's offset 0x18 reported above:

```
$ aarch64-linux-gnu-objdump -s -j .rodata key_injector.ko

key_injector.ko:     file format elf64-littleaarch64

Contents of section .rodata:
 0000 6b65795f 696e6a65 63746f72 5f696e69  key_injector_ini
 0010 74000000 00000000 24ccd690 79643e83  t.......$...yd>.
 0020 35e2d8db bf81cb54 ad365b79 8c53993b  5......T.6[y.S.;
 0030 3fc7fb73 d8574209 6b65795f 696e6a65  ?..s.WB.key_inje
 0040 63746f72 5f657869 7400              ctor_exit.
```

And we can see that the desired data are the 32 bytes at offset 0x18, that is, 24ccd690 79643e83 35e2d8db bf81cb54 ad365b79 8c53993b 3fc7fb73 d8574209.